HOW TO LEAD A BADASS BUSINESS FROM YOUR HEART

The Permission You've Been Waiting for to Birth Your Vision and Spread Your Glitter in the World

HOW TO LEAD A BADASS BUSINESS FROM YOUR HEART

*The Permission You've Been Waiting for
to Birth Your Vision and Spread Your
Glitter in the World*

Makenzie Marzluff

CHANGEMAKERS
BOOKS

Winchester, UK
Washington, USA

JOHN HUNT PUBLISHING

First published by Changemakers Books, 2021
Changemakers Books is an imprint of John Hunt Publishing Ltd., No. 3 East Street,
Alresford, Hampshire SO24 9EE, UK
office@jhpbooks.com
www.johnhuntpublishing.com
www.changemakers-books.com

For distributor details and how to order please visit the 'Ordering' section on our website.

Text copyright: Makenzie Marzluff 2020

ISBN: 978 1 78904 636 6
978 1 78904 637 3 (ebook)
Library of Congress Control Number: 2020938306

All rights reserved. Except for brief quotations in critical articles or reviews, no part of this
book may be reproduced in any manner without prior written permission from the publishers.

The rights of Makenzie Marzluff as author have been asserted in accordance with the Copyright,
Designs and Patents Act 1988.

A CIP catalogue record for this book is available from the British Library.

Design: Stuart Davies

UK: Printed and bound by CPI Group (UK) Ltd, Croydon, CR0 4YY
Printed in North America by CPI GPS partners

We operate a distinctive and ethical publishing philosophy in
all areas of our business, from our global network of authors to
production and worldwide distribution.

Contents

Dedicated To
All of the visions ready to fully birth onto
this planet.
Thank you for trusting me with this message.
And thank you for always finding me when you need someone
to have your back.

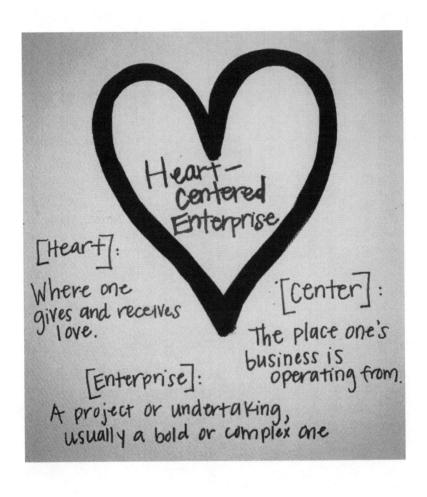

Preface

A Book about Business and Playing Big

I finished the initial draft of my book in 2018, and already so much has changed. Every month I am being invited into deeper mastery of something new when it comes to business, so I bring to you this book having mastered only what I speak about in the pages ahead. I am constantly being "promoted" to my next level of mastery, and I am committed to not teaching anything before I've really risen through it.

Every business has various phases. This book speaks mostly to the phase of your business journey that represents the battlefield, or what the I Ching would call, *the difficulty at the beginning.* This is the part of your life and business where you are thrown into the trenches. Where you are taught what true surrender means. Where you are confronted with every ounce of self-doubt, lack mentality, and ancestral wounding that keeps you from *living* your true vision and soul's calling.

This is the part of the journey where you learn that you are on this planet to be thrown into the fire in order to make real and lasting change, and where you are confronted with every part of you that resists that fire.

This is the part of the journey where you own your creative power, and you get in the birthing position to actually bring your creations into the world. This is where you push, scream, and cry of both pain, surrender, bliss and gratitude.

I have come out of this part of the battle, proud and strong. And I'm most proud to say that not only do I have a successful business, but that I officially love the fire. Every day, even when I am scared, I stand up and allow life to hit me. The good, the bad, the ugly. I have finally chosen to run into the battlefield because fighting for love is so worth it... and honestly, now that I look at it this way, it doesn't actually feel like a battlefield at all.

I am grateful for all of the lessons that have led me here. I feel abundant, prosperous, connected, purposeful, inspired, creative, strong, fearless, and capable. It doesn't mean I don't have tough days—it means I lean into the tough days with curiosity and courage. Mother Earth has provided for me in ways I never could have imagined, and I am finally able to claim that I deserve it.

I have two beautiful babies—or entities, as we call them here. Delighted By ("DB") and KAKAO. Both were started on my credit cards, and now both are thriving, debt free. In just five years DB sold $15 million worth of dessert hummus (damn!), my team has grown, and my leadership has finally blossomed. And it's all been done *from the heart, in ways that go against everything we learn in traditional business school.*

I often say that conscious business is one of the greatest platforms for personal development that exists. My businesses have been and continue to be my teachers. I've been in one crazy bootcamp the last five years and now it's time I pass on much of what I have learned.

On a final note here, I want to share how much my body resisted bringing this book to life at first. I realized how easy it had become to hide behind my entities. To bring my *own voice* through and shine in a new way for our tribe was confronting to say the least. I was faced with a solar plexus upgrade that required purging cellular self-doubt, fraud syndrome, "who am I?" syndrome, fear of rejection, fear of losing my humility, and more than anything: fear of feeling separate from my community by stepping into this new level of leadership. As I went through deep ceremonies of releasing these blocks to my leadership, I contemplated writing about it on Instagram so that I didn't have to publish a book. It would be quicker, easier, *smaller*. I wrote a post a bit back that ended up holding me deeply accountable through this process. Accountable to offering my life lessons forward in a more permanent, stickier, and bigger way.

Turning my suffering into Art. This is my greatest value these days. It is the secret to many of the great musicians, poets, writers and visionaries. Very rarely do I turn my suffering into Instagram posts, because posts are gone in a flash. The greatest gift I can ever give the world is to turn my moments of breakdown, my periods of suffering, and deepest shadows into something tangible that lives onward. It's why Logic's #1 Best Selling Novel was written during one of the darkest, most anxious and painful parts of his life. It's why the book that Michael is writing about Sex right now is an actual living transmission of all he is experiencing in real-time, especially the most painful and confronting days. One day you'll get to hold that book in your hands, and it will impact the next generations of boys that will become men. KAKAO as we know it today has been birthed through betrayal, confusion and heartbreak — and when you hold your cup of KAKAO each day you have my entire journey of healing and re-opening right in the palm of your hands. I have turned rejection and life-shattering reflections of greed into an Event that will hopefully lay entirely new business templates across the globe. Two weeks ago, Michael and I were evicted from our home that we had just moved in to, and after hitting my knees on the floor and confronting my own wounding and worry-patterning, we are now birthing a KAKAO Ambassador program that will have genuine impact on communities, and Delighted By... my beloved DB. She was birthed after intense years of depression, confronting all the loss, unworthiness and severe fear of intimacy I had taken from my childhood. I may not be a poet, but my businesses and offerings are indeed my poetry. Thank you, Instagram, for your constant access to connecting with my friends, but I will never waste my precious suffering and therefore my sacred creative force on explaining my healing journey in a post. The most integral thing I can do for myself is to honor my suffering by feeling it, loving it, and then standing up yet again to serve. Turning my suffering into Art. This is my greatest value these days (**@kakaodrinkingchocolate**).

I now come to you with a finished product in a place of deep knowing that I am the one meant to deliver this message. I am tremendously passionate for not only these codes, but for the next generation of entrepreneurs like myself. I am willing to do anything possible to bring this wisdom to you through embodiment, and to keep going until it's complete. My soul is asking me to take the torch and to start marching, in the name of business itself.

So here we go! Gather yo' crystals, your cup of KAKAO, maybe your fave essential oil, and follow me.

Key Concepts and Terminology

D elighted By (DB): The physical expression of "Delighted By" is a vegan, gluten-free dessert company that sells dessert-dips and other healthier treats to retail grocery stores across the United States. We are the inventors of the original "dessert hummus" — a dip made from chickpeas in sweet flavors. The formal business name is Delighted By Hummus LLC, which we have since rebranded as *DELIGHTED BY: Desserts Worth Sharing*.

Delighted By is also referred to in this book as the invisible energetic being "DB" which is the entity I talk to, write to, ask for guidance from, and be led by within all of the business's operations. DB is a feminine entity, so you will hear me say words like "she" and "her" when speaking about DB.

Entity: Every business has an invisible energy behind the actual physical manifestation. This energy I call an "entity." This is not to be confused with the word entity that some people in the spiritual community reference as something negative that latches onto you or is meant to be "cleared." In the case of what I write about in this book, it is similar to how human beings also have a Soul, an invisible energy we refer to when speaking of our truest essence. DB is the soul of my business, and I confide in her when making all decisions. If you have a business, you too can tap into the "soul" of that business—the energetic life force behind it that has a mission and has decided to express itself through products, services or some other expression.

Ceremonial-Grade Cacao: Cacao is the raw form of cocoa, which is used to make chocolate as you know it today. Ceremonial-Grade cacao refers to a unique, wild strain of cacao that is sourced only from countries who grow cacao natively without any hybridization or genetic modification. In addition to sourcing native strains, ceremonial-grade cacao entails using non-industrial methods of producing (such as stone-grinders) in order to use the *whole bean,* which western chocolate companies rarely do anymore. This protects the vibration of the cacao itself. Ceremonial-Grade Cacao is consumed in the form of a hot, creamy drink and used in "ceremony" where the intention is to open the hearts of those participating. In these ceremonies, repressed emotions come to the surface for healing, connection is formed amongst the group, and creative energy is sparked. Ceremonial-grade cacao is also used on an individual level for daily meditation, journaling, creativity, focus, or any other intentional practice that connects one with their Higher Self.

KAKAO: Short for KAKAO Ceremonial Drinking Chocolate, a 501c3 not-for-profit organization that sources native strains of cacao above fair-trade price, working directly with partners on the ground in Peru, turning it into the ceremonial-grade cacao product mentioned in the previous paragraph. KAKAO's mission is to open the hearts of the Western World by making true ceremonial-grade cacao accessible, and in doing so also assist in protecting the native strains of cacao (and therefore the farmers involved), which are indeed endangered in both Peru and Guatemala.

Conscious Enterprise: A way of running your business with awareness of yourself, your fears, your anxieties; a new paradigm of business that is free from competition, unconscious "doing," and greed; a way of operating from a pure place of service, while also dreaming big and receiving everything your heart genuinely desires; a spiritual approach to all aspects of business that leaves you feeling connected to something greater than your singular self.

Light-worker: An individual who is tuned into a higher way of living and leading and utilizes their life and all its expressions as a way of shining light into others and into the world. An individual who works with light and focuses on the light through the way they live and serve. A light-worker could be a healer, business-owner, photographer, writer, speaker, mother, and everything in between. If you are here to BE your light, use your light, and create more light in the world, you are a light-worker.

Higher Guidance: Another way of saying intuition, or gut. Some people call this Spirit, Source, God, Goddess, Universe, etc. Others say, "Inner Guidance" or "Inner Knowing."

Gaia: The spirit of Mother Earth. Just like every human has a soul, our planet Earth is a living being with a soul herself—which we call Gaia. Gaia is a wise, ancient, beloved sister across all the star-races and she willingly provided herself as the physical planet on which we humans would experience, transform, and ultimately ascend. In my visions, Gaia's true spirit form is a white and gold dragon. Gaia speaks wisdom into me about every area of life, especially business. Gaia is my main spirit guide, which is why I refer to her often in this book: I like to give credit where credit is due.

Guides: Or Spirit Guides. There is a world of beings beyond the human eye that is witnessing us and furthermore, supporting us. When we develop our intuition and detox our bodies from society's conditioning that keeps us blocked from our intuitive power, we can begin to see, hear or feel our Guides. For some of us they can be in the form of angels, ascended masters, animals, minerals or star-beings. Being connected to the "other side of the veil" in this way is our birthright as human beings.

Plant Medicine: Plants, used as medicine, whether it be for physical, emotional, psychological or spiritual healing. There are thousands of plants in the jungle of South America and from all parts of the world that are intended for healing purposes, some of which induce what one may call a "psychedelic" experience, and others that are not psychoactive. Some of the most commonly talked about plant medicines in our culture now include Ayahuasca, San Pedro, Peyote, Cacao, Psilocybin and Ibogaine, to name a few.

Ayahuasca: A plant-medicine primarily found in the Peruvian jungle, brewed into the form of a tea for healing purposes. After going through vast preparation and cleansing, the tea is drank under supervision and guidance of a trusted Shaman, where the human then communes with the spirit of Ayahuasca and can go through vast amounts of healing and transformation. In this book, I may refer to the Ayahuasca as "the medicine," "Madre" or "Aya."

Gene Keys: A body of work by Richard Rudd, more specifically a "living transmission" that includes Books, Online Programs and Audios to support one's journey in diving deep into their genetic makeup (their DNA) through the pathway of their Shadow, in order to unlock their deeper Gifts. The Gene Keys is rooted in the wisdom of the I Ching, as some people have experienced through the body of work called Human Design. The Gene Keys, and specifically the "Golden Path Program" takes you on a journey of activating your genius, peeling back the layers of your heart, and stepping fully into your prosperous path of bringing your gifts to the world. The Gene Keys work has been important for me in integrating all of my work with plant medicines into everyday life. To get your free hologenetic profile and begin working with the Gene Keys, visit www.genekeys. com.

Primal Fear: An energy that lies deep within our DNA

from lifetimes of wounding. Our primal fears are rooted in survivorship—fear of not having enough and therefore fear of dying. At its worst, primal fear in business expresses itself as greed, corruption and selfish hierarchal modals. At its best, primal fear is transcended by the entrepreneur by being felt, forgiven, released and transformed into an energy of love, oneness and heart-centered leadership.

Zone of Genius: A phrase originally used by Gay Hendricks in his book *The Big Leap*. Your zone of genius is your creative essence. The expression of your soul that you came here to express. Your soul signature within your business. A natural expression for you that feels like artwork in the making. Your Zone of Genius is expressed spontaneously, naturally, and with delight that is deeply fulfilling. Residing in your zone of genius leaves you feeling energized, tapped in and connected to the whole—as opposed to burnt out, drained and disconnected from Self.

Channel: A vessel for which something from the higher realms can come through, whether it be wisdom, a message, or even a song. Every one of us has the opportunity to become a clear Channel for their soul's light in all of its various expressions. I channel my entities DB and KAKAO, as well as other creative projects that flow through effortlessly. When your channel is open, light can pour through for the betterment of humanity.

Divine Feminine: Soft, in flow, nurturing, feeling, expressing, communing, worshiping, devoting, mothering, connecting, caring, creating; mysterious, no one direction, diverse.

Divine Masculine: structured, focused, linear, clear, concise, strong, space holding, truth, presence, directive, action, love.

5D Consciousness: Another way of saying Unity Consciousness. A realm where magic is possible, where universal love is all there is, and where heaven really IS here on Earth.

Sovereignty: Clear in oneself, knowing what and who is good for you, rooted in self-worth, healthy boundaries, integrity with true self, free from limiting beliefs or systems.

KAPU: An app, created by Michael McPherson and Makenzie Marzluff, to provide a safe and sacred space for like-hearted humans to connect online. Through regular virtual cacao ceremonies, wisdom offerings, and written shares, you will develop meaningful friendships with other empaths and light-workers that are on a mission to restore balance on Mother Earth. KAPU can be found on iTunes and Google Play. Learn more at www.joinkapu.com.

Introduction

The Conscious Entrepreneur's Creed

The concepts I rap about in this book can't be taught through simple words. Everything that I wrote about here came from my Higher Guidance—from Spirit/ Source/God/Universe/My Womb—call it what you want. These messages have often come through Plant Medicines (such as Ayahuasca and Ceremonial Cacao), from Mother Earth herself, and from my other guides/helpers of course. Delighted By is also a guide for me in a way, as she (my business/"entity") does guide me through this process. Not to mention, she is the platform on which I have learned most of what is in the pages ahead. She has been my driving force to learn and embody conscious enterprise. In result, I have received so much more than a thriving business—I've received *me*, the woman I always wanted to be.

I am sharing this information with you because Delighted By and KAKAO told me to. I was guided to hold this space and to share what I've learned, taken away, and experienced thus far on this magical journey. But like I said, these principles can't be taught by me; they have to be *felt* in you. Embodying conscious enterprise is going to come from *your* guidance. To embody the new paradigm of business is really going to come from a *feeling*. And the only way you can feel something is by checking in with yourself. You can read a book; you can hear a speech; you can read my words. But if you don't actually let it hit your cells experientially and from your own inner wisdom, it won't stick.

If something worked for me, it doesn't necessarily mean it's going to work for you. What I experienced along the way doesn't actually need to be experienced that exact way for you. Just keep this in mind as I am sharing. At the end of some chapters I have a Q&A section to address the frequently asked questions when I share such information through my speaking, coaching or other programs for entrepreneurs.

If you have more questions that come up for you, it's an opportunity to check in with *your* guidance. May you be reminded often throughout this journey together to check in with your own personal alignment.

When it comes to your unique vision, know that it's going to happen no matter what. Your vision IS coming to life, period. My intention is to share my experiences and all that I have learned thus far in hopes that you can have a little more fun along the way. I know your vision feels really big, and at times unachievable, yet you can rest assured that its coming into physical reality has already been written in the stars. My goal is that you are happy and delighted along the way of its unfolding, in a place of ease and grace.

Before I get into sharing my story, I want to pass along *The Conscious Entrepreneur's Creed,* something I channeled a couple of years ago. The Creed is a list of affirmations and commitments that you can say to yourself or keep somewhere as a reminder throughout your journey. Conscious Enterprise does not simply mean "triple bottom line" anymore. Triple bottom line is when a business has social, environmental and economic impact—that's what people have described as conscious enterprise in the past. But to me, conscious enterprise is now so many steps beyond that. It's deeper, led from the heart, and with the opportunity to have great impact on an interpersonal level. So, when someone asks me, "What does conscious enterprise mean to you?" It means the embodiment of this Creed.

For each concept, I elaborate further in the chapters of this book. This Creed will give you a framework of where we are headed in the pages ahead, within which I will elaborate on each statement that this Creed contains.

The Conscious Entrepreneur's Creed
Read these as if you are the one that wrote them.

#1: I Lead from My Intuition
I tap into my own guidance and choose to be a true, clear channel for the vision desiring to birth through me.

As a leader and business owner, my *intuition* is the sole decision maker, as opposed to my mind.

I trust my inner guidance by *getting out of my own way* and embracing a greater wisdom that comes through me, specifically through my heart.

I lead with these questions daily:
What would you have me say?
What would you have me do?
Where would you have me go?

Even in new situations and uncharted waters, I rely on my guidance to lead every step of the way.

When others challenge me with their way of seeing it, no matter what their credibility may be, I still come back to *my* guidance system and make sure I lead only when I get a resounding yes from within.

#2: I Am the Embodiment of Unity Consciousness, Leaving Any Sense of Competition at the Door

In my conscious business, I do not act from a place of competition because I am tapped into the truth that we are *one family*. I believe that all businesses should be run with this foundation of Unity engrained into its DNA.

When I see others offering similar services or products as me, I simply choose to not give any attention to it other than celebration. "One Family" means that *my wins are their wins and their wins are my wins.* There is so much abundance available to us that we can literally *all win.* There are endless amounts of customers, creativity, bliss, joy, celebration, delight and resources.

This lifetime is about everyone winning, so I stay conscious of where any fear may seep in when so-called "competition" arises. I simply re-shift my focus to my unique vision and bring it through in a high-vibe, service-oriented way for the greater good of all.

I trust that my vision chose me, and that it is my responsibility to channel it through from a pure and inspired place that is true to me.

My business that is birthed on a foundation of unity and collaboration is an integral pathway to changing the world for good.

#3: I Am in Personal Alignment and Balance

In this new paradigm of business, I know that there is no need to self-sacrifice.

I really *can* have it all—not just a thriving business, but also thriving health, relationships and other passion projects.

My entity desires alignment in every area of life; if I fall out of alignment (i.e. not enough sleep; not enough self-care; overworking; "doing" things within the business that don't feel in my highest joy etc.), my business will reflect it. The more I allow and receive alignment in every single area of my life, the easier business comes, the quicker my vision blossoms, and the more fun I have along the way.

#4: I Make Zero Decisions from Fear

Every time I make a decision, I ask myself, "am I making this out of fear or from a place of trust and love?"

I move forward with my aligned ideas, knowing that I am always provided for.

I acknowledge that the old paradigm of business has carried primal fear from generation to generation, therefore I see my business as an opportunity to align my financial spreadsheets and decisions with spiritual truths and heart-centered leadership.

I also recognize some fear as a good thing, knowing that taking big risks and new leaps is absolutely required of me in order to bring my vision to life. I use fear as a guidepost in this way.

I embrace a sense of trust in the universe knowing that when I act from love, I will always be caught.

#5: I Have a Personal and Ongoing Relationship with My Business Entity

A deep, intimate relationship with my entity (the invisible energy behind the actual physical manifestation of my business) is my solid foundation for growing my vision. My entity has its own distinguished energy, or life form. *I* am not my entity; *I* am not my business, but rather I am the humble servant of the vision itself.

My relationship with my entity continues to deepen and flourish the more that I commune with her/him. I converse with her/him; I ask questions; connect with; experience; delight in; be curious with; and learn from her/him regularly.

Embracing a deep relationship with my entity greatly helps

my journey of bringing my vision to life in the most intimate, guided and ease-filled way.

#6: I Am 100% Authentic and Transparent, which Includes My Vulnerability

I am transparent about everything. I am real about when I mess up; I am real about how my business operates and why. I am bold about who I am, and when fear comes up inside of me, I work through it honestly and fully.

I recognize that people can *feel* the transparency and authenticity of my brand, products and services. They can feel the motives and intentions behind my company simply by scrolling the Instagram account and visiting my website. Customers may not have the language for it, but they can *feel vibrationally* that my company is one they want to support with their dollar.

In addition to being transparent and authentic, I embrace vulnerability as a strength in all of my business relationships, whether it's with team members, investors, customers etc. I lead with my heart forward, meaning I always speak my absolute truth even if I am nervous. I set my ego aside by letting go of worrying about what others think, and I bring my authentic feelings and emotions forward when they are present for me. I acknowledge that speaking vulnerably to my true life experience is what brings me in closer relationship with everyone in my life, including those connected to my business. I encourage a work environment and culture where vulnerability is embraced and celebrated.

#7: I Have a Sacred Relationship with Money

I believe that abundance is my divine birthright and therefore my decisions are never made from a place of lack. I acknowledge and feel in my cells that there *is an endless supply of abundance.* I commit to working through any limiting belief systems around the topic of money.

I choose to invest my personal and company's resources consciously, meaning I bring intention to every decision where we circulate money—whether it's to a team member, supplier, marketing effort etc. I see our resources as sacred and I honor the flow of those resources, whether it's in or out. I honor that currency is meant to be like a healthy current of water—never stagnant, always flowing.

I value myself as the Chief Channel of my business, and therefore receive compensation that feels good to me. I allow my compensation to evolve depending on the stage of my business. I am surrendered to the way my business interacts with the energy of money.

#8: I Am a Full Yes

No matter how scared I may become, I am a *full yes* to my vision and to all the steps my entity asks me to take for my vision to come to life. I open-heartedly claim that I am here, I am a yes, and I am ready. I understand that the business may bring various challenges and tests, but I am committed. I am asking to be a part of something that is greater than me, therefore it will require a level of complete surrender to the divine plan as well as the action it will require to carry that plan out.

#9: I Reside in My Zone of Genius

To be in my zone of genius means to only do what I was *born to do.*

My zone of genius mostly includes the things that I am naturally good at, and that which I am truly delighted by in this life.

There are aspects of my business that are an opportunity for me to express my zone of genius.

There are other aspects of my business that are *not* my zone of genius, therefore I delegate them out whenever possible. I acknowledge when I am being invited out of certain roles and tasks and therefore, I hire out other people that are in *their* zone of genius.

I consistently evaluate what parts I am meant to be involved in, and what parts I am meant to *stay the hell out of.* Every week my role changes in my business, because as my entity grows and/or evolves I am instructed on my particular involvement.

#10: I Operate from a Calm Nervous System

My nervous system is my greatest asset in my business.

I bring awareness to my breath in every moment possible.

I embrace lifestyle choices that support a calm nervous system, and I make a conscious effort to get into nature every single day.

Every action of my business is embraced ceremonially, meaning I bring intention and breath into every email, communication, decision and creation.

I catch myself when I am rushing and I consciously slow down.

When I act or speak from an overstimulated nervous system, I take responsibility for it and acknowledge it to anyone who may have been impacted.

Taking inspired action in my business from a place of calm and clarity always produces the greatest long-term results.

Now, let's dive deeper into these concepts and play together in this epic world of conscious business that you are at the forefront of creating!

Chapter 1

Spread Your Glitter

To come to a place where I can courageously pioneer new ways of operating business and lead 100% from my heart's guidance has required me to go through a journey of tremendous healing and many "initiations" as I call them. I am assuming that if you're reading this, the same applies to you.

I grew up in Dayton, OH USA, a highly conservative town as you can imagine. I was "accidentally" conceived by two beautiful souls at their young ages of 19 and 20, who then divorced when I was four years old. My parents were wounded, as many parents of our generation are, and they didn't have the tools or permission to heal emotionally the way my generation does. For my mother, this unhealed wounding expressed itself as extremely controlling and emotionally unstable, which was only accentuated when we joined the Christian Church. For my father, his unhealed wounds were expressed through cocaine addiction. My mother was physically there but it was a hostile and abusive environment that greatly impacted my ability to use my voice, have confidence, or embrace my free spirit. I became a people-pleaser with a good-girl identity that wanted to make my Mom and grandparents proud. My father was not there physically for various reasons, and this lack of presence was the greatest heartbreak of my early life. It impacted all of my relationships, my ability to connect intimately, my body confidence, and more. I say none of this to blame or be a victim of my upbringing; I have deep reverence for all the soul contracts here and know that everyone is doing the *very best* they can. With that said, the truth is that I was impacted and that it needed (and deserved) healing. I'm beyond thankful for it, because it has led me to where I am today, and now my relationship to these family members is free from any of my own resentment, anger or grief. I say with a full, genuine and healed heart: thank you Mom and Dad for choosing on a soul level to go on this earth-walk with me so that I could be the person I am today who is sitting here writing this book.

It was in college that I began tapping into the desire to find myself; to really know who I was and what *my* belief systems were. As I started to explore the college life like any college student does (boys and booze included), my mom was not pleased, especially due to the fact that most of it I would try to hide or lie about out of my fear of getting in trouble. At the age of 19, I was separated from my mother, my sister, my brother, my adopted father, all of my grandparents, my cousins, and my aunts and uncles through a very traumatic and physical event that occurred between my mother and I. I was cut out from literally my entire family, as the event was re-created for my family members in an untruthful way that made me out to be the mentally unstable one. This didn't feel very loving, at all. This gave me ammunition to *not* be spiritual or religious because I started associating God with judgment, fear, shame, and the opposite of love.

During this time, I was doing the best I could to stay positive. I had many moments of struggle for sure, but overall, I was a pretty positive person. I went to college in Arizona, so the sunshine was always out—I enjoyed the weather, the nature, being creative, and I worked a lot. I was getting through with my mindset, "everything is going to be fine." I had big dreams— and now that I wasn't in contact with the family members who wanted me to behave in a certain way, I could now live "however I wanted to" without fear of getting in trouble.

One semester before graduation I decided to leave school and fly to Australia. I wanted to get as far away as possible and explore something different for myself. I went to Australia with the intention of being there for a semester, but I ended up staying for two and a half years. I was in a romantic relationship with an Australian, and I started my first business as a Holistic Health Coach very shortly after moving to Sydney. I stood outside of a health-food store and asked every single walker-by if they would like a free nutrition consultation. I got a lot of noes and some yeses; and over the course of one year I built up an entire nutrition coaching practice and a full database of clients. I eventually opened *Glow Nutrition & Pilates Centre,* which was an intimate and sweet space in Surry Hills; we had 42 Reformer Pilates classes per week, cooking classes, and nutrition programs. It was really, really fun. However, I still was not tapped into my true spirituality, and I had a slew of inner child work and healing that I needed to go through—I just didn't know it at the time! I had a very limiting belief system around money that was rooted in lack, and even though my business was doing really well on the inside of those doors, the minute I walked outside of them I was pretty unhappy. I was struggling internally while I was there, but to the outside world it looked like I had this awesome life. I blamed Australia for my unhappiness, so I came up with a plan to leave. I sold my business, moved back to Phoenix, AZ, and ended the romantic relationship I had been in. In hindsight it was my soul leading me of course. I had a lot of growth to do and apparently Phoenix was going to be the place that would kickstart it all.

In Arizona I started another business venture fairly quickly. For another two and a half years I worked on a venture called *Osaka Sun Blendery,* a plant-based smoothie drive-thru concept. It was a concept that in the end didn't end up fully birthing; things weren't flowing how I expected them to, but I was learning tons in the process. What I was learning most is that *it doesn't work to force things.* At the time I didn't have any of this language in terms of "talking to my entity" or even the word "abundance." After forcing and struggling with bringing *Osaka Sun Blendery* to life, I finally walked away from it all together once I accepted that it wasn't meant to happen. Throughout this time, I was also in a rather karmic, toxic romantic relationship. This relationship ended up being my rock-bottom at the end of it all, the thing that propelled me into what most call the dark night of the soul. Throughout those couple of years there were ups and downs, breakups and makeups, cheating, fighting... you get the picture. Over time, I began realizing that every time we fought, I would hit the floor and *really miss my mom and dad.* At the time I was not in touch with my mother, and while I had been in contact with my biological father for the first time in over ten years, it wasn't the true father-daughter relationship that I had always yearned for with him. The little girl inside of me never had any kind of healing around either of these relationships. I would hit these challenging moments and wish that my mom and dad were there. So over time, it was clear that my relationship with Zachary was meant to bring up all my "inner child stuff" and all the issues I still had around my parents so that I could actually *heal those wounds.* After breaking up for what I thought was the final time, I found out that I had fallen pregnant. Z looked at me as if for the first time he had felt a sense of purpose in his life; I saw how happy and excited he was to hear this news. So, I decided to move forward with the pregnancy and we moved back in together. I honestly thought my life and big dreams were over at this point. I had never wanted to be a mom (at the time) and I just wanted my business to come to life, so I felt trapped, nonetheless. Once we moved back in together, we started fighting even more. It was extremely unhealthy and emotionally abusive (for both of us) to the point where I had to make the shocking and traumatic call to have an abortion. At the time for me this was devastating; it was something I never, ever thought I could bring myself to do. But it was really clear; even though I wasn't consciously tapping into my higher guidance back then, looking back I can see that it was indeed Spirit telling me, "you have to get yourself out of this situation." I just knew, finally, that being connected to this relationship in my current less-than-healed state was not in alignment. I heard clearly, "It's time to get out and to choose you."

I remember having the procedure. It was very traumatizing, and that's when things really started getting bad for me. Now I'm trying to get over this relationship, I have a bit of mini-PTSD plus tons of shame from the abortion, and my business venture *Osaka Sun Blendery* was put to rest. I was having nightmares; I was barely sleeping; I was extremely stressed, and it got to the point where I was so depressed that I didn't even want to be on the planet anymore. I was genuinely contemplating suicide. I literally couldn't even recognize myself. I thought, "I've been through everything—stuff with my Dad since I was little and a horrible falling out with my mom and family, yet I had still been okay." But now this, it took me to a true rock-bottom. It was a scary time, and I had no choice but to fall to my knees in that moment. A good friend told me, "You have to be determined to get yourself back." Little did I know that not only was I going to get myself back, but I was actually going to get my *real self* for the first time in my life. This is late 2014.

I now have a free bedroom available, and thanks to the Divine, it was filled by a roommate that I found on Craigslist named Dulce. Dulce was incredible; she was balanced; she practiced yoga and meditation; she was genuinely embodied in her spirituality but not in a better-than-thou way. She was really solid, to the point where I looked at her almost a bit envious, and even slightly embarrassed because I felt like I didn't have anything to offer her in my current state. However, I knew deep down that I needed her energy and good influence around.

The first time we sat down to have dinner together, I started crying to her—which I really hadn't ever done with someone before, especially with a stranger. I told her I was struggling with getting over Zachary, I was struggling from the abortion and the guilt of it, and that I was having very negative (suicidal) thoughts about my entire existence. Dulce came over to me and said something that literally changed my life forever.

"Oh, baby girl, you just need some momma love."

Huh. I hadn't even told her yet that my mom was not in my life. So, I thought, "maybe she's about to give me a hug, some momma love or something?"

But instead she looked at me and said, "You know what you're going to do? You're going to give that momma love to yourself. Go into that bathroom, look down at your body, and say, I'm going to heal you. I'm going to protect you; take care of you; comfort you; re-mother you."

This advice forever changed my life, to say the least. Dulce then introduced me to Louise Hay, the author of *You Can Heal Your Life*, which then led me to Mirror Therapy. Immediately that day, and weeks following, I began looking at myself in the mirror. Initially it was really tough for me. I couldn't even look myself in the eyes, which was confronting in itself. If I can't look myself in the eyes, how can I look anyone else in the eyes? I wanted to not only be able to look myself in the eyes, but to be able to look at myself and say, "I love you," and mean it. I had to work on this for a while. I was following Louise Hay's guidance with her affirmations of wellbeing and self-love; I was reading everything Dulce recommended, i.e. *A Return to Love* by Marianne Williamson, *Spirit Junkie* by Gabrielle Bernstein, *A*

Course in Miracles, and more. I was also journaling affirmations and all my thoughts, dreams, hopes and feelings.

One day when looking in the mirror I surprised myself by being able to look myself in the eyes and say, "I love you." What happened in that moment was nothing short of miraculous. All of a sudden, I saw my five-year-old self in the mirror. There she was, standing before me, like she had been waiting for me to see her—*actually* see her. And she told me everything she wanted to hear—essentially all the things she had not heard from her mom and dad.

You're beautiful.

I'm so proud of you.

You can't do anything wrong.

You have a heart of gold.

You've got this.

I'm going to take care of you.

I'm going to protect you.

All the things that she had never heard, but really needed to. She wanted *me* to tell them to her. So, I started doing that in the mirror even more; affirming, re-mothering, re-parenting. Loving up on her, on that little girl, on myself, and saying, "I Love You" and really meaning it. I was on a journey of Self-Love. This was my "pre-work," and this journey of self-love itself brought me out of my depression and into a much better, clearer place.

In January 2015 I received a phone call from an old friend who I hadn't seen in a long time. He told me he was going to an Ayahuasca ceremony and that there were two spots left. He asked me if I wanted to go… *that night.* I had never heard of Ayahuasca; I had next to zero experiences with mind-altering substances outside of alcohol; but for some reason I said yes, very quickly.

For those of you that haven't worked with Ayahuasca, quick note: She is a feminine plant spirit; people refer to her as Madre, or Mother Ayahuasca. She comes in the form of a tea, which once consumed, can deliver under the proper circumstances profound healing on a physical, mental, emotional and spiritual level.

Aya found me, rather than me having to seek her out. I had not prepared consciously but looking back I can see that Aya had been preparing me with the inner child work, mirror therapy, spiritual books and the positive influences I was attracting into my life. I had never read *anything* about Aya, but now I was in my friend's car, on the way to Sedona, to sit with Ayahuasca for the first time. David said to me, "All you need to do is set your intention."

I told David that my intentions for the ceremony were to release anything from my past relationship that I hadn't released yet and to know what my purpose in life was. My questions were, *What is my purpose? Why am I even here?* And, *What am I supposed to do with this life?*

In my first Ayahuasca ceremony, I was totally won over. For those that haven't experienced this plant-medicine, you may view Ayahuasca simply as a mind-altering substance for healing purposes. But once you actually sit with Ayahuasca, you realize that it doesn't feel like an "it" but rather a "she." Just like I refer to my business DB as a she, a separate entity, I also refer to Aya in this book in the way it's true for me: a feminine, motherly energy that I have a profound relationship with. From my first ceremony onwards, she began speaking to me and delivering messages.

The first message I received from her, in my first ceremony was, *Makenzie, your purpose is to spread your glitter.*

Or in other words, to *be* the light that I am. I heard, *It doesn't matter what you do, but more so how you do it. Simply bring your energy and light to every room and person you come into contact with, and in that you will spread your glitter and therefore fulfill your purpose.*

This gave me a huge sense of relief. I had been raised in a household where traditional success, money and status (school, education, stable job, etc.) was encouraged. Doing, striving, and achieving was glorified. Masculine energy was glorified; Feminine *feeling* and creating was avoided and shamed. So, this divine message from Aya herself gave me this sense of relief that I no longer have to worry about doing, I can just *be*. In simply *being me*, I will spread my glitter, and in that I will fulfill my purpose.

I went home the next morning in a total state of peace and bliss; my life had literally changed in the course of twelve hours. I remember getting another big message to *never* write another business plan again and let go of all the ways I had operated business in the past. For the record, I am naturally entrepreneurial, Delighted By being my fourth venture, KAKAO being my fifth. So, I had some experience with business plans and operating from the "old paradigm" as we call it here. I remember talking to my Aunt Amy on the phone after my ceremony and she asked, "So, what are you going to do now?" I said, "Well, I know what I am *not* going to do, and that's write another business plan. I'm just going to see what unfolds naturally from here, day by day, moment by moment."

That night, eight hours after the completion of my first ceremony, I was making my dessert hummus—which I had started making the year before just for fun. As I was making it, I heard *another message*. I was literally stirring the chocolate chips in, staring at it, and I heard, *This is one way you're going to spread your glitter.*

Dessert hummus? Really? Yes, really... I was being told to bring this product to the world and use it as a vehicle to spread my glitter.

I literally woke up the next day, went to the Maricopa County Health Department to obtain food permits, and was at farmers' markets within a week for my new company, *Delighted By Hummus*. My mission with Delighted By from day one was to inspire people to spread *their* glitter. I loved asking people, *What are you delighted by today?* Because when we do more of what we are delighted by in life, we in result spread our glitter and fulfill our unique purpose.

What are you genuinely delighted by in life? Can you take radical responsibility for your life by only doing the work you are delighted by? Only surrounding yourself with people you are delighted by? And ditching all the obligations, societal pressures and expectations that you *aren't* delighted by in order to be of greater service to the world? The only way you can truly spread your glitter in the world and be an earth-angel of light is by following your delight, through and through. Set all previous glorification of traditional success aside and give yourself over to the image of you sharing your light and love with the world in every way you possibly can before you leave this Earth. Bring extra awareness to your energy field the next time you interact with someone or the next time you step into a room. Beam your delight into the room and let those around you bask in your being. You can spread your glitter to the cars you pass on the highway, to the team members you're in a meeting with, or to your family members at the dinner table. You can spread your glitter through the emails you write, the creations you channel, and the businesses you lead. It doesn't matter *what* you do, but more so *how* you do it—in a state of delight and in a way that spreads your glitter according to your divine blueprint.

Chapter 2

Mastery in Intuition Is the New Master's in Business

Accessing your Higher Guidance is the key to bringing through your incredible vision. You know that you have this beautiful purpose and that you're here to really leave a legacy. And your vision, your entity, chose you because it trusted you to follow through with it until the very end. It trusted you to leave a lasting legacy that's truly going to impact the planet in a positive way. Your entity chose you *now* because it's time to lay energetic blueprints, or *templates,* of heart-led businesses across the globe.

I believe that when we restore the heart into big and small business, our world will change. Those holding money and power in a conscious way (you and me) will move resources to where it's needed most, restoring balance on our planet as a whole. I believe that if you're reading this book, you were chosen to be a part of this restoration. I believe that the businesses we create today will indeed lay the foundation for generations to come, and that we must do things very differently than our society was conditioned to do.

Now that you know why this work is so important, I want to teach you the simplest and most essential tool you'll need to play your part in leaving this legacy of love through your business.

Up until working with Ayahuasca, the concept of "God" or anything "bigger than me" freaked me out because of my religious upbringing and everything that happened between my family and I. When my roommate Dulce would mention God in conversation, she'd remind me, "When I say God, I'm really just implying your Higher Self." This helped because it gave me context that I was comfortable with. When I read *Spirit Junkie* by Gabrielle Bernstein, the words she used often, "Spirit, Guide Me," became engrained into my being. And then coming out on the other side of my first Ayahuasca ceremony, I had zero qualms anymore about referencing the God of love that I know internally. This first ceremony had me recognize and accept that clearly there is something bigger at play working here, and from there I connected in deeper with an expression of spirituality that felt aligned for me. So, I took this knowing, this deep connection to God/Spirit/my Higher Self, and I began using it in my business from the very beginning.

The phrase, "Spirit, guide me..." was one that was playing in my head with nearly everything I did, big or small. When I went to Hobby Lobby to buy my table items for the farmers' market, I said "Spirit, guide me." When I went to the health department to get my food permits, I said, "Spirit, guide me." When I walked up to my first farmers' market, I said, "Spirit, guide me."

Spirit... What do you want me to buy? How do you want this brand to look? How do you want this to come to life?

I stayed curious and asked a lot of questions. By asking for guidance, I was allowing myself to be *the channel*. The channel for Delighted By, the entity, to come through me naturally and divinely. I was turning on my creative tap so that DB could flood through, without my ego or mind getting in the way.

I remember walking up to my first farmers' market, super nervous but excited. I was by myself and I said to myself, "Spirit, I ask that you guide me today. I ask that you speak through me, I ask that you work through me. This is my intention." And then boom, it all started from there.

One of my intentions for starting in farmers' markets was to get proof of concept for my dessert hummus. I knew that my friends loved my product, but I wanted to find out if others would. I was also curious... *why in the world has no one created dessert hummus yet?* Within three months of farmers' markets, we were selling out at every single event. I grew out of my own personal kitchen making hummus in six Vitamix machines, all burning out because you're not technically meant to run a Vitamix for eight hours straight. I always asked Spirit to turn it back on, of course. We transitioned into a commercial kitchen space quickly. I then received guidance to raise some capital, which is when I started applying to *ABC's Shark Tank*. It was February of 2015 that I started Delighted By in farmers' markets. By May 2015 I left farmers' markets because my big vision from Day 1 was to be the first dessert hummus to *national* shelves. I stayed focused on the big vision even though I had a lot of people at the time telling me to stay in farmers' markets while I scaled up and grew the business organically. But for me, the farmers' markets took too much energy away from my bigger vision. Now that I had proven the concept of dessert hummus on a smaller scale, it was now time for me to shift focus completely on the bigness I knew I was meant to bring through.

A big part of asking for guidance is *listening intently and trusting what you hear.* Even when and if everyone else isn't fully on board with you. I want you to fully grasp how beautiful and clear something can be when you simply *ask for guidance.*

When I started this venture, I knew nothing about the food industry. I had no idea what it would take to bring a product from my kitchen to the shelves, and I didn't know anybody who had done so before. To make things more promising, I had zero money. I started Delighted By on my credit cards. I didn't work part-time when I started Delighted By—no, I went all in from day one. I just knew that's what it was going to require. All in, day one.

Disclaimer: I am not implying this is what I recommend you do. I talk more about this specific topic in the Q&A section of Chapter 3. For now, I want to share my story with you exactly as it unfolded for me.

After the farmers' market test, I downsized to a suitcase and went on a nationwide search to find a manufacturer that could make my dessert hummus without preservatives.

In May 2016, one year after leaving farmers' markets, we finally launched to shelves. For this launch, I lived out of a van that I rented for four months, traveling up and down the east coast with coolers of hummus. I slept on those coolers. It was a pretty crazy yet beautiful time, as I kept asking, "Spirit, guide me." I continued my work with Ayahuasca every month, which offered tremendous mentorship, healing, guidance and empowerment to me along the way. Aya assisted me in tapping into a greater body of wisdom that contributed to most decisions I made in the business. And she taught me on a cellular level about the art of surrender, despite all the discomfort that the journey held.

To give you more of a glimpse into this timeline, I want you to know that as I sit here today just a few years after launching to shelves, Delighted By is in around 5000 stores nationwide. It's now a team of ten and growing. And I have done it all by honestly and truly *following my guidance.* Which is why I feel that obtaining your Mastery in Intuition is the new Master's in Business. I may not have a formal MBA, but I certainly feel qualified to lead entrepreneurs in discovering a new way to go about business because all I really need to do is direct them to their own guidance system.

All that you need to start your business or lead your existing business in a completely new way, is already inside of you. All of the wisdom, guidance and tools are sitting right inside of your sacred vessel that we call a human body. And you don't even need friends or family around you that support this way of doing business. In fact, you can expect most people to think you are a bit crazy. You can expect to be challenged by the modern business world in your perspectives and the concepts outlined in this book. That certainly was the case for me.

When I started my journey, I didn't have a "tribe" yet or a network of likeminded people that could rap about this spiritual approach to business. Of course, I had family members supporting me through that time, which I am so grateful for, but I was out there by myself doing the actual work and discovering what conscious enterprise truly means. I was going to ceremonies, living in my van, seeking out knowledge and mentorship, researching, making calls, knocking retailers' doors down, and working to bring my vision through, completely on my own. Shoot, I didn't even have a personal Instagram account for the *first four* years of my business. You know what that's called? *Focus.* I share this because sometimes starting something new, or pioneering new ways of operating, is a lonely ride for a while. No one knew what dessert hummus was, and many people looked at me like I was crazy for trying to bring this new product into the food industry. I didn't have a platform to speak from, and I certainly did not know a single other person talking about business the way I was. I was being taught about a totally new paradigm of operating business in my Ayahuasca ceremonies, and for a long time I kept most of it to myself. For me it wasn't about sharing the message, it was about *embodying* the message through my business. DB was giving me on-the-court opportunities to practice what I was learning, and really no one was there telling me it would turn out okay, other than Aya herself. It was all based on a gut feeling and a true commitment to following my guidance, which honestly felt extremely risky most of the time.

I was scared shitless when I rented that van and decided to drive up and down the east coast promoting my product, especially after everyone told me I shouldn't do it. I genuinely was scared most days, but now I have learned through those experiences that fear is a powerful guidepost. Every time I lean into my fear, a miracle occurs. I am now connected to a ride-or-die tribe that I never could have dreamed up. I now feel more supported than I ever even knew was possible! But it wasn't until I started *practicing and embodying* the new way of business, did all the real miracles come. I was going for it. I was uncomfortable 99% of the time. When I went for it and said to the Universe "yes, yes, yes" over and over again, even when I was scared shitless, *that's* when the capital and funding showed up; that's when the tribe of support showed up; that's when the company started to really move and grow.

I won't lie to you. Entities with a mission to restore the heart on our planet in one way or another may ask you to do some things that are indeed pretty uncomfortable. As you develop your intuition and begin hearing guidance regarding next steps to take, you may be pretty shocked at what you're being asked to do. You could be told that it's time to quit your day job in order to pursue your venture full time. You may be asked to end a business relationship when you don't have another partner in place at the time. You may be asked to walk away from an investment deal with Mark Cuban (that happened). You may be asked to live out of a van for four months, sleeping on coolers of hummus and driving thousands of miles across the country. You may be asked to let go of an employee. The possibilities are endless, and it's your responsibility as the conscious entrepreneur to trust your guidance and act on it in the timing being asked of you.

We are always 100% safe to act from our intuitive guidance,

but our bodies may not know that. Our brains are wired to fight-or-flight programming, and our nervous systems are wired to support that programming. So, it goes without saying that your neurological pathways and brain chemistry will get several upgrades over the course of your business career when you're committed to the new paradigm. We can support this re-programming by speaking to our inner child, by doing mirror therapy, with affirmations, and by telling our brains and bodies, "Thank you for trying to protect me, but I am reminding you now that you are 100% safe to move forward."

Over time, making big decisions that are seemingly scary will become more natural for you, meaning you won't feel as scared. The more practice you have, the easier it will become. Remember this the next time you hear intuitively to make a scary decision. Use that opportunity to practice and remind your brain and body that it can expect nothing but miracles to unfold post-decision. Miracles are always mysterious in that you never know what they will look like exactly. But you can always expect them, and most importantly, you should look for them.

There is a soul contract between you and your entity, meaning you said yes to partnering with your entity long before you reincarnated as a physical human being. Your soul made a decision to be an open, clear space of service to your entity, and in return to receive all of your wildest dreams come true— for yourself and for the planet. The contract between you and your entity is not something to take lightly. In fact, it deserves reverence and respect! You chose to be of service in such a powerful way in this lifetime, and therefore you can trust that everything is always working out for you and your entity.

In the beginning, before you start talking to your entity, before you start worrying about money, before you start facing all of your fears, and before you even do more inner child work, you have to start with asking for guidance. That's how you get from here to there: by asking for the guidance as much as you possibly can.

Ask your guidance system: where would you have me go? What would you have me say? What would you have me do? Practice this with everything. Ask when you're ordering food. Ask when you're writing a post on social media. Ask when you're about to speak. Ask when you're driving somewhere. Ask for the guidance in every opportunity possible so that you can develop your intuition at lightning speed.

An entity that is meant to help heal Mother Earth and humanity needs to be able to trust that you'll bring her/him through 100% in alignment to *their* vision and their purpose, all personal agendas aside. They have to be able to trust that you will genuinely lay a solid foundation for them to leave the legacy that they are here for. If they don't trust you, or if you don't trust yourself, they will have no choice but to hop on over to the next person that will honor them fully. You do not need to be perfect by any means in order to be the channel that these kinds of 5D entities can flow through, but it's important that you're committed to being open, bold, in alignment, authentic, willing to surrender, willing to trust, and willing to get out of your own way. And above all, you have to be willing to develop and surrender into leading from your intuition.

Energetically, I put a filter around this book. Therefore, the only people that are drawn to this book are the ones that are 100% committed to bringing through a fierce, beautiful, *big* vision that's literally going to lay the foundation of the next shift in consciousness for our planet. Those are the kind of people that I invited into this work. And that's *you*. So, it's super important that you master this "asking for guidance" thing and the ultimate willingness to surrender. There is so much help available to us, which I've had to learn the hard way.

Madre Ayahuasca showed me countless times just how often I get in my head about things and therefore block all the help that is available to me. With a challenging situation in my business I would sometimes think that I need to "figure it out," diving in and doing it all on my own. But then I realized, if I would just stop, pause, open my hands, relax my shoulders, and breathe deeply, staying in the discomfort but really *still,* then this signals my Guides to all come in—to heal my body, to reset my nervous system, to adjust my cells, to adjust my brain chemistry, to remind me of the Truth, to send me loving frequencies, and to strengthen my backup. This protocol I just listed here is absolutely needed if you are an empath in business with a big vision. Look, if you have a massive vision with extraterrestrial energy like Steve Jobs or Elon Musk, and your soul isn't here to have deep relationships, hold compassionate space for the Planet, or do it in an extra-conscious way, that's one thing. But *you,* the people reading this book—not only do you have a vision that you want to see out, but you also are the empaths of the world. Meaning you feel *everything.* And it's because you feel everything that you're so committed to healing everything, within yourself and therefore the collective. So, in working with an entity, you can expect to feel *a lot* of emotions throughout the journey because that's what you came here to do!

This is why I don't call myself the CEO. I was given another title early on in my journey: *Chief Breath-Taker.* My main "job" is to breathe. Sure, I may do other tasks (obviously) but all that really matters is that I am breathing fully, deeply, and consistently. DB has told me through Aya many times, "you are the breath of this company." So, I take this role pretty seriously. As soon as I am doing something that shortens my breath, taps my nervous system, or feels out of alignment, I stop. I breathe. I ask for guidance. Asking for guidance is the key to being receptive to all of the divine help available to us. And breath is the quickest way to get there.

No one can tell you what's aligned for your business other than you. Any action that you take needs to be inspired, or in other words, guided. For me, there are times where I am inspired and guided to work all day. And then there are times where I am inspired and guided to not work at all, i.e. be off technology completely. Whatever it is that I am being guided to, I have to own it regardless of what my brain says about it. If I am inspired to work for twelve hours straight but then I complain afterwards, then I just took away my power and the choice that I had in working for that long. Which by the way I have done many times on my journey with DB... #human. What I have become better at over time is listening to my true inspired guidance, choosing to follow it, and then owning it without guilt. If I am guided to channel my Divine Masculine energy one day, then I must honor my masculine side and the way I can organize, have powerful communications, and provide structure for my organization. And then there are days (more so than ever) where my Divine Feminine side needs balancing out. She'll say, "I just need you to be gentle with yourself. Rest, go get a massage, get outside." But she'll say it on a *Tuesday*. My brain goes, *wtf? We have production, deliveries, team meetings, blah blah blah.* And then my heart comes back in and I just own it. I tell my team what I am being guided to and that they probably won't hear from me much that day. "Let me know if you need anything. I love you guys. You got this!" It requires a huge amount of trust, that's for sure.

The difference between Delighted By and my past ventures, is that my past businesses were primarily ran from my masculine *mind* and I'd say a sense of force. I was more focused on what I "thought" should be done and "figuring out the how." Whereas with Delighted By, it's been a more surrendered, feminine, balanced flow, leading from my heart's guidance rather than my mind. It doesn't mean I don't take actions. Everyone in my life can attest to just how much action I have taken and continue to take, but it's simply coming from a different and more balanced energy.

You don't need to sit with Ayahuasca to reprogram your brain—you can do it right here and now! Set your intention, ask for the angels to assist, and surrender to the process. Begin to notice where you overthink things and call on the guidance to soften you back into your heart.

Our protocols as conscious entrepreneurs to breathe, be balanced and receive energetic support are pertinent in bringing a big vision to life. Especially because our businesses are not going to happen overnight. It took Delighted By over an entire year after the farmers' market launch to actually get to grocery store shelves, which honestly felt like forever to me. And still, we have *a lot* more we want to accomplish! In the process of it all coming to life, soul contracts play out in business partnerships, team members, retailers and more, contributing to the overall multi-layered mission that DB holds.

Honoring your entity means honoring its timing, and really delighting in the entire process. You can't only get caught up in the end vision, but instead acknowledge that every single moment of the journey is sacred and meaningful. The goal isn't to get from here to there per se as much as it is to allow it all to unfold and embrace the timing as divine. For instance, if today you are impacting a few people with your message, service or product, but all you worry about each day is wanting to impact millions of people, then in a way you just failed to acknowledge how sacred the two, three, or even hundreds of people are. You must acknowledge that your entity and your soul are up to something big and *every step of the way* is important. The timing of it all is really pre-destined, so it comes down to how much you choose to enjoy the journey. How much are you going to choose to honor the timing? To honor its sacredness rather than just wanting to speed it up all the time? It is so important to dream big, absolutely, but please do not turn your dreaming into resistance of the present moment.

On a similar note, don't doubt the divine wisdom of your entity. He/she knows exactly what she is doing, and *always* has a divine reason for the timing they choose. In fact, if you stay present enough, you'll experience the true miracles that are unfolding in those precious moments. Your entities have so much more up their sleeve than just the "vision" themselves. They have people, souls, vibrations, and hearts that they are intending to impact *every step of the way.* As you ask for your guidance, *always look for the miracle that your entity is conjuring up.* Staying connected to the sacredness of the mission is an integral part of conscious enterprise.

I have one more grand story for you on following guidance. In November of 2015 I was living out of a suitcase and had been working on DB for about nine months thus far. Because of my relationship with Ayahuasca and fascination with plant medicines in general, I researched them in my down time. I wanted to learn more about all plant-medicines and how they could have such a powerful impact on consciousness and how we operate in daily life. While I was reading about shamanism, anthropology, the Amazon Jungle, and medicinal properties of different plants, I kept coming across the word "cacao." It kept jumping off the page at me. Obviously being in the food industry and being someone that loves chocolate, I was quite intrigued at the fact that the word Cacao was very apparently trying to get my attention.

In general, I was curious about potential plant-medicines that could be used on a more daily basis, which then I could share with my friends and family. Ayahuasca had been so powerful for me, and at the same time I had this feeling within me that there *must* be a gentler (and socially accepted) plant medicine that also has similar effects. Cacao jumping off on the page was Her way of saying, "yes, there is something, keep looking."

I started researching everything I could on cacao. I discovered that the Mayans have been drinking cacao (chocolate) for centuries, and that they've been doing so with a very specific strain of cacao—the native strain, called Criollo in Guatemala and Chuncho in Peru—for both spiritual and health benefits.

I discovered that there was such a thing as a cacao ceremony. Extremely interested, I then discovered the Chocolate Shaman named Keith who lives in Guatemala. On his web pages he refers to cacao as the Royal Cacao Deva, in others words a "plant goddess." He was speaking about her as if she was Ayahuasca. Highly intrigued, I ordered some from him. It took a month and a half to get to me and it arrived in the form of a solid block. I had to figure out what to do with it—and finally read that I had to chop it up, weigh it out, and add my sweetener of choice, plus some vanilla, chile and hot water. I read that to have a cacao ceremony, you are to set your intention, bless the cacao, and invite the cacao spirit into your heart.

Cacao ceremony #1. I am solo. I do everything listed above. And boom, to my surprise, she took over my entire body. I wasn't expecting that because, "it's just cacao," I thought. I was laying there on my yoga mat completely in awe. I fell in love with her that first day because of the way I felt her open my heart and the incredible vibration pulsing through my body. As I started working with her a couple of times per week, I became more connected to my Higher Self, to others, to nature, and to my vision with DB. I was becoming more creative. I noticed that the cacao started fueling my days while working on Delighted By, which ended up being what completely got me through my Van Tour.

Right when I drank the cacao for the first time, this vision came to me from Cacao herself. She showed me that one day I was going to bring this ceremonial cacao to the world in a bigger way. But I was left in the dark of how or when that would happen, as acquiring ceremonial-grade cacao was a pretty challenging feat to my understanding.

I started sharing cacao with friends, family and strangers in my travels with DB. They would love the experience and always ask, "how can I get some?" As soon I walked them through the complicated and lengthy process of ordering, chopping and whisking, they would look at me like that was never going to happen. Clearly the process of obtaining and working ceremonial-grade cacao into daily life was way too complicated for the average person. This reinforced my desire to bring ceremonial cacao to the western world in a more accessible way. But I had no idea if that would even be possible. It was clear that no one had done it before. No one had brought in true native cacao. At this time, I had brought myself up to speed on to what true native cacao means and saw that no one had brought native cacao, in drinking form, to the states.

I assumed this vision of bringing ceremonial-grade cacao to the USA, which was present with me in the winter of 2015 and early 2016, was several years down the road. It was very much a "one day" kind of thing.

In June 2016 I was at a trade show for Delighted By, and when I came back to the Airbnb that night with my team member, I heard a message from my inner guidance. "It's time to go to Guatemala."

My brain: *What do you mean it's time to go to Guatemala?*

Guidance: *It's time to go pursue this cacao venture; it's time to figure out how to get the western world cacao. Now.*

My brain: *I'm still not financially ahead by any means. I'm still trying to get Delighted By off the ground and onto shelves. I'm super deep in DB right now. There is no way this is possible.*

I said to my team member, "I just heard a message that I am meant to book a flight to Guatemala to explore the cacao project."

My team member: "I think you should do it."

Scared shitless, I booked a flight that night on my credit card, which was set to leave about two months later. Honestly, I couldn't believe that I did it. In August 2016, I flew to Guatemala for a ten-day trip with the intention of finding out, one, why has no one done this yet? And two, can I even get my hands on enough native cacao to consistently import into the USA?

I went to the Chocolate Shaman's ceremonies in Lake Atitlan

to learn more about what cacao ceremony means to them. I then found out about a lady in Antigua who makes cacao, who many people were telling me about. I eventually showed up at her doorstep, and when I walked inside, she said, "I've been waiting for you. I knew someone was coming from the States to talk to me about my cacao."

Clear guidance, yes. The cacao spirit was indeed talking to me, yes.

And now here we are. I launched KAKAO Ceremonial Drinking Chocolate in January 2017, which months later become an official 501c3 not-for-profit. When I was in Guatemala that first time, I fell in love with the Guatemalan people—I totally respected their way of being. They don't have a lot, but yet they're still so happy. KAKAO never was intended as a way to make money, so I thought why not reinvest the profits back into the farmers and community? This mission magnified when my partner and Beloved Michael came on board. We were guided to source cacao beans directly and make the drinking chocolate in-house to ensure the integrity and consistency of our product. In this process we discovered just how challenging it is to source native cacao, and how much of a need there is to protect what are essentially endangered strains of cacao by increasing the demand and keeping a transparent, ethical supply chain from start to finish. The reason is that the commercial chocolate market has placed pressure and demand for the modified, hybrid strains of cacao that are easier to control and cultivate for the huge market demands. In turn, the wild, native strains are much more expensive, and the farmers aren't as incentivized to harvest them due to low demand. We were blessed with a partner in Peru, Matt, to ethically source native Peruvian cacao in a strain called Cacao Chuncho, which is now our main cacao source and one we feel tremendously connected to.

I share this part of the story to have you understand that even though I was really scared, and even though I had no idea how it was all going to come together, I simply followed my moment-to-moment guidance. And now, what a gift! We have this beautiful entity KAKAO that is one of the greatest passions in my life. It has brought Michael and I together in such a beautiful, creative way, and it has connected us to our best friends and soul family across the globe. It is one of the greatest joys of our life to get you all this sacred cacao. And on top of that, to know how the increased demand KAKAO has contributed to the farmers of Cacao Chuncho, is a true honor.

It's incredible what can be created when you stay in your alignment by listening to your intuitive guidance and pioneering heart-centered enterprise with your unique ventures. And that is why I wanted to write this book. I just had to share these stories. I had to show you all that it really does work. I am sure many of you already know that and are in the actual experience of it, but if there is ever a doubt in your mind, i.e. "Does this whole Love thing really work? This whole Higher Guidance thing? This whole believing in Abundance thing? This whole entity-connection thing?" You can come back to these stories and remember, *Yes, it actually does work.*

May this inspire you to always, always follow your guidance, no matter how scared you are.

Here are a few questions that I received from the community when beginning to talk about conscious business and acting from intuition.

Q&A
Q: How do I know if I'm getting guidance?
A: This is a challenging concept to describe, whether it's to someone in the spiritual community or not. To understand what true guidance is, it is important for you to distinguish your conditioned mind and/or ego from your true internal guidance system.

Guidance typically *feels* right, although it may not make much logical sense in the moment. This doesn't mean it won't be scary but trust me when I say it always feels right to you from deep within your belly. It may be guiding you to "plug your nose and jump," aka take that scary leap, but it should feel scary in a good way.

If it feels bad, negative, low-level, or skeptical, *that is not your guidance system, that is your mind.*

Your mind or ego can at times try to keep you small, simply to keep you safe. Your higher guidance will always lead you to a place of bigness and empowerment. That's not to say, however, you won't be guided to practical, informed decisions in your life and business, but you will maintain a level of awareness, or as some say, consciousness of leading from this intuitive place.

You ask, close your eyes, quiet your mind, and listen. Then depending on your unique makeup, you will get a ping in the form of a gut feeling, a visual, a sense of knowing, or a voice that you know is not your ego. Meditating or going into nature for long periods of time can help you connect to your inner compass, or in other words, your guidance system.

Q: What's the best tool for connecting to my guidance system?

A: Oh, there are so many ways, from meditation, to being in nature, to dancing on your own. Ask to be guided to the ways and tools that are best for you. The most important thing in developing your guidance system is to set aside time each day to be in silence and stillness. By silence, I mean a space where all the noise of the world is tuned out. You may still be listening to some soothing meditation music, for instance, but all other media, phone communications and distractions are closed out in order to fully tune into *you*. By stillness, I mean inner stillness. You may still be walking, dancing, or practicing yoga—but you have attempted to still your mind and calm your nervous system. It's in this type of silence and stillness that you can truly connect with your higher guidance.

I personally love to write, and I find massive benefit from it. I journal a lot. if you look at my journal entries, it's a bunch of letters that start with:

Dear Spirit,

Dear God,

Dear Higher Self/Soul,

Dear Gaia/Mother Earth,

Dear Inner Child,

Dear Delighted By,

In these letters, I ask for guidance. I ask a lot of questions and even share my thoughts and feelings. From there, I set an intention to fully get out of my way and allow a higher wisdom to come through my pen. This looks like me asking that higher wisdom to speak through the pen, answering whatever questions I may have posed. This may sound like an odd concept, but it can be developed by anyone over time. All it takes is practice and consistency. Elisa Romeo, the author of *Meet Your Soul*, teaches how to do this in depth through her concept she calls *soul journaling*.

Q: When do you hear your guidance?

A: When I get quiet.

In my daily Cacao Ceremony.

When I move my body. Moving meditation is a real thing.

When I'm in Nature.

When I meditate or sit in stillness.

When I write.

When I'm in water (i.e. shower, bath, ocean and a float tank).

When I make love to my Beloved.

Chapter 3

Relationship with Your Entity

In one of my earlier Ayahuasca ceremonies in 2015, Delighted By presented herself. A feminine, purple spirit, and she just started talking to me. I realized then that DB is different than me and that she can offer me guidance.

My relationship with DB is intimate and personal. Knowing that DB is a guiding force reminds me that I don't need to rescue her or that I am here to teach her, but rather she is a mirror, a mentor, a friend, a sister to me. Referring to DB as a confidante has tremendously assisted me, especially when challenge and contrast arises. When I feel DB's energy, it honestly can be pretty intense at times and only something I can take in doses as per the alignment of my body and nervous system. Knowing that she is an entity that has a unique plan allows me to soften into her strong energy, and furthermore, to deeply receive her. Her intense energy is actually something that can be received as pleasure and playfulness, as long as I stay open, curious, and in full conscious breath.

If you look at your entity as a business, you may think *I have to figure this out. I have to wake up each day and "work" on it. I have to do this and that for my business.*

If you look at your entity as a separate being that you have a relationship with, you'll be more inclined to:

Chat to your entity.

Ask questions.

Stay curious.

Communicate your personal preferences.

Recognize that it is not all on you, but rather it is a partnership with your entity, and furthermore, that your entity is moving through you.

I have written dozens, maybe hundreds of letters to Delighted By along the journey. My relationship with her has been all over the place. As I look back on the letters I have written her, I observe a plethora of emotions in the various stages of the business. In the beginning, there was so much honor. *Whatever you need from me. I love you. You're amazing. I'm at your service.* Another phase: *What are you doing? What in the world are you up to?* In a challenge, weak and surrendered: *Dear Delighted By, Dear Delighted By, Dear Delighted By...* with no idea what to do and attempting to reconnect with her.

I notice that when I write to Delighted By, she writes back to me through my pen. Entities all have different energies. Some may be more masculine or feminine, and some may not have an associated gender. Delighted By feels very loving; she feels quirky, funny, light-hearted; she feels very fierce in the most badass, Goddess way, which always inspires me to step into that more. She is really mysterious in a way, which is why I am constantly asking her what she is up to. She is always revealing different pages of the book that I wouldn't have expected. And she is a constant invitation into unconditional love.

She is so confident. She doesn't care what other people think or how other people may have done it in the past. She's like, *Whatever, we all know where we are going here.*

It's very clear that all of my entities are *not me*. You may pick up on my opinions towards them, but not a personal identity to them. Your entity does not have to feel like mine. They all feel very different and they all come from different realms. You can communicate with your entity about your preferences. If you are in a relationship with your entity, know that they absolutely do want you to have self-care. They have a lot of respect and honor for you in that you said yes to them. You can trust and surrender to your entity. You can ask for what you need. You can tell them how you're feeling, and they will listen. They will get it, and they will most likely offer you vast amounts of wisdom.

For much of my journey, I struggled between channeling my business 24/7 with honoring my soul's alignment and personal balance. I learned over time that our entities do not require us to grind to the point of sacrificing our health and happiness. Which is why I say *the grind is dead.* Your entities can be up to incredible things, but that doesn't mean it has to be demanding on you to a point of misalignment. If you feel any demands on you, know that's coming from *you*, not your entity. Your entities are so loving, and while they will bring you to places of surrender, learning to trust more, and learning to ask better questions, they would never ask you to do something that isn't in alignment for you.

I look back at the most challenging moments of my business and remember how overwhelming it was for me. I now know that DB was initiating me in many ways. She was teaching me about breath, she was teaching me about calling on the invisible support all around me, and she was leading me to my dreams in ways I didn't know were necessary. Looking back, I see how each point of intensity was indeed necessary, for it always led to something beautiful.

If you're saying yes to your vision, channeling your entity with willingness, and then shit hits the fan in your business in one way or another, your first step is to stop and breathe.

No matter how many affirmations or videos on the Law of Attraction you listen to, it won't replace the fact that you need to let the energy of your entity run through you. Let the energy of your entity be pleasurable, even fun. I have learned to be less uptight about DB's energy, and just let her flow through me as the creative force that she is. Love your entity for that, and also remember that you can tell your entity if you prefer something different. It's a two-way relationship.

Again, your entity would not ask you to do something or feel something that is not in your highest and best. Entities just want to play. They already know where they are going and what's going to unfold. They already know the end game, so in the meantime they just want to play, delight and have fun. I lived out of a van for four months with seven coolers of dessert hummus, traveling up and down the east coast while launching DB into stores. That was us playing together. That was us locking arms, having a blast of a time. Sleeping on coolers, laughing when the cops banged on the window one night from being in a wrong parking spot, almost getting towed while sleeping inside, brushing my teeth inside of Starbucks, showering in gyms, and listening to a lot of rap music. When I look back at it, that was DB and I being in the full experience of our friendship. There have been times where I haven't chosen to look at it as play, so she asks me, "Would you prefer to go back into the van?" Implying that if I don't choose to look at everything as play, she will bring me back into a place or situation that will evoke that energy from me. The entities are truly friends that desire to play and create together while leaving a legacy of love for the world at the same time.

Curiosity is key with your entity. When your entity challenges you, asking the right questions is going to help you have less resistance. And in fact, you'll get to see more clearly the miracles on the other side of every challenge!

Three weeks after launching to grocery stores for the first time, my chocolate chip hummus began molding on the shelves. The customers were purchasing hummus that already had mold on it. In shelf-life studies, this flavor had exceeded 70 days shelf-life in a controlled environment. But in a situation where temperature was less controlled (several warehouses, transportation, retailer fridges, etc.), it was going bad at 37 days.

I had to pull all of the product off the shelf and not get paid for it. I thought that maybe it was a one-off thing, where a truck wasn't cold enough or something. So, I had my manufacturer re-make it. I sent it to the distributor... and it unfortunately happened again. The chocolate chips were absorbing moisture from the chickpeas, which was causing the mold.

I was then faced with a very tough decision. In order to maintain our values of not using preservatives or mold inhibitors in our product, I chose to discontinue the flavor all together. This was our top flavor, and essentially the flavor that launched my company. But I knew it was the right thing to do, so with lots of tears I pulled the trigger on discontinuation.

In the end, this situation led to a few miracles. When I made the choice to discontinue the Chocolate Chip Hummus, I set out to create a flavor that was just as good if not better. I flew to Boston and went into product development right away, completely determined to birth something super special. The result? Our Vanilla Bean Hummus, which I will never stop feeling like a super proud momma for (especially when my Beloved Michael eats an entire tub in one sitting, with a finger). The second miracle associated with this challenge is that it led to My Aunt Amy and Sozie (that's what I call my grandmother) to being shareholders in Delighted By. I share this story in detail in Chapter 4, but for now just hear me when I say that when you stay curious with your entity, miracles flow.

Many times, entities are up to Soul work. Meaning they have a soul contract with another individual, and from their big, beautiful hearts of service, they put this into their divine blueprint. Entities are often always wanting to be in deep service, to the point where they're not concerned how it appears to impact them—because they're so solid in who they are and the truth of it all. It's *our* humanness that gets scared about credit holds and steep bills that we don't know how to pay. But our entities know that an overdue $35K bill is nothing in comparison to the opportunity of inviting my own blood family into her Operating Agreement. This soul contract is priceless.

Many times, she is trying to do Soul work with others too: our manufacturer; other team members; and beyond. She has many soul contracts laid out on her map that I am constantly catching up to. Even just today I was in a new realization of a soul agreement between Delighted By and one of her employees that isn't necessarily the same soul agreement between this person and myself. Entities have behind-the-scenes soul contracts with humans, beyond only yourself (the channel). You can make your life a lot easier when you fully grasp this truth and allow it without kicking and screaming all the time.

When practicing this level of conscious enterprise, there can be tons of shit that goes down that no one will ever know about. These soul contracts between entities and our planet are so sacred, and unrelated to their direct product/service/brand, that the general public will never even know about it. Even my family members, investors, and close friends don't know all the stories; and my employees certainly don't even know the start of it. As a humble servant to an entity, it's important to understand the sacredness of the behind-the-scenes work they do. They have infinite layers to them.

Delighted By is so much more than just hummus. The public will never understand what I really mean when I say, "it's not just about hummus." They think, "oh, she means it's about spreading her glitter like she always talks about." They think that when I say, "it's more than hummus," that I am implying DB is about an expression of creativity. While DB is in many ways a massive expression of me spreading my glitter and the desire to inspire others to do so, it's actually much deeper than that. My experience of DB as an organization is one that involves soul work most people won't ever know about or understand. To sit in partnership with DB each day is a ceremony in itself. She does soul work with corporate buyers of large retail chains; she does soul work with our investors; she does soul work with our employees, ex-employees and brokers; and obviously she does soul work with me.

When you say yes to an entity and yes to being a channel, you're being of massive service because you're really giving the foundation for your entity to be of service in a bigger way. Even when that soul work creates a bit of "wtf" in you at times. Entities require deep surrender. Sometimes it's super uncomfortable. This is when it's time for you to soften and open. And when you do, there is always a beautiful message and/or gift there.

I like to use sex as an analogy. If you're anything like me (especially if you're female), entering into the sex space requires surrender, softening and opening. And if you're anything like me, sometimes that can be kind of challenging, to the point where you want to avoid it and tense up. But, when you actually do surrender, with every part of you, mind-body-spirit, you *fully receive*.

Same thing with business and with entities. When you surrender fully, you receive. When you let go, and completely soften with open hands, open body, you receive gifts such as divine guidance, miracles, abundance, connection and love. No matter what your entity and/or message is, there is always a bigger picture that you can remember you are a key part of. You and your entity are working together to leave a lasting legacy. Allow yourself to step into the bigness of this and over time your fears about money, what others think, or the potential of failing will melt away. Surrender to the vision itself because that vision is indeed bigger than you, and it has a divine blueprint for how it will all play out. *Your* responsibility is your happiness, health, relationships, and nervous system along the way.

I see entrepreneurs (including myself) all the time getting very attached to the current status of their business and vision that it robs them from enjoying the gift of life itself. You have a handful of divine birthrights, including bliss, love, and abundance—so let's stop robbing ourselves of our very own birthrights. We can do this by realizing that our entities and our visions are up to their own path and own timing. It is not in our control, so let's surrender to that and meanwhile claim back what *is* our control, which is our attitude and our perspective.

Many entrepreneurs believe that their entity has to come with lots of difficulties and roadblocks so to speak. Nope! My perspective is that entities are divinely intelligent, so they believe in a thing I call *framework*. Humans, however, *think* that they don't want or need framework. They think they want the big massive vision all at one time… quickly. But thankfully, our entities are a lot smarter than us.

Our entities know that our bodies and nervous systems need and deserve one step to come at a time. Our entities know that our visions need and deserve the proper learnings, wisdom, team members, and foundation for them to thrive long-term. And this is why I talk about the word Surrender over and over again. I don't speak about surrender because you are necessarily going to go through a zillion grueling days. I speak about surrender because your entity has a plan that deserves to be trusted, fully. I speak about surrender because your vision needs you to be calm, positive, clear, full of breath, and blissfully thriving.

Recap: When your entity isn't moving as fast as you'd like, it's because they're laying down framework. Your job is to surrender to their timing by *thriving through the process.*

Shit, sometimes while I am managing ten employees and a seven-figure national business, I miss those simple days in the van passing out single tubs of hummus to store managers (and homeless people). I mean, not really... but my point is, I'm so grateful for the framework. At the time, I was dreaming of my hummus being in every single store within three months. When our chocolate chip hummus spoiled on the shelves, I was so grateful for the framework. When we have logistical issues, I am so grateful for the framework. When I have to let go of an employee, I am so grateful for the framework. And don't forget all the incredible people you will meet along the way as this framework gets laid. Like when I was knee-deep in credit card debt and an angel investor handed me a check for $20K. That's framework, or in other words the divine wisdom of our entities. (More on this story in Chapter 3.) Thank God I wasn't a trust-fund baby who was all comfy while launching this brand, because I would have missed out on some of the most fulfilling relationships, including all of my investors. I would be missing out on some of the most fulfilling memories and stories of how those relationships came to be. In another instance, we have had challenges with our manufacturer in terms of making product on time, or batches that turned out less than perfect. But from these situations came deepened relationships with the executives and team members within that organization. Our entities' framework is a gift, simple as that. If you experience a roadblock, you can choose to see it as a difficulty or as the *pure wisdom of your entity.*

A message from your entity:

You are tremendously supported. There are invisible helpers and also soul family (earth-angels) that I will be revealing on the path along the way. There are gifts, messages and downloads that will come through without you even needing to look for it. I have your back. I have set up pre-destined support long before you even heard my voice. Let's fly!

Examples of Letters to My Entities:

Dear Delighted By,

Thank you for the magic, your friendship and your love. You play to my strengths and for that I am grateful. I trust you. I trust that you are in alignment with your purpose and you will continue to be. I love that you chose Wegmans as your first retailer and it is beautiful to see it unfold. That really brought out my youth and opened my heart wide open. I tap into divine wisdom to guide me for these next steps, to take us where you need to be next. I surrender. I bring healing to the planet. I am of help and service. I listen to where you need me to go. I get quiet before I take action.

* * *

Dear Delighted By,
It's been a lot of letters. A lot of ceremonies. Oh, look at what you brought me. The gift of you... has been me. In you, through you, I discovered me. Every challenge has been and is a sacred opportunity to grow, learn, practice, experience. Look at what you have infused into my DNA, into my bones. Look at what you did. I will never be perfect, but I'm a whole lot more aligned thanks to you. Thank you for your service to me. Through you, I discovered the truth. The freedom, love, delight and abundance of all of this. You gave me an opportunity to be of service. We made quite the team, huh. And certainly, some funny memories :) Thank you for trusting me. For connecting me to my guides, Aya, higher self and inner child. Thank you for always having my back. Thank you for your godly patience with me. Thank you for connecting me to soul family and so many incredible people. Thank you for being just so perfect, cute, delicious, delightful, badass, unique, magnetic, interesting, heart-opening, funny and mysterious. I always knew where this was going. And here we are. I know we will always be with each other. Thank you for being softer with me in these last moments. Thank you for every single moment of expansion. I love you.

* * *

Delighted By,
What intention should I hold? What vision should be in my heart
and eye? What would you have me do, say, how do I lead? How do
I keep your intention as alive as possible? How do I be a vessel for
the soul work on the large scale that you do? Please deliver me your
guidance, please show me the vision. I am listening and looking.
Look how far we've come. It's been one hell of a ride. I'm truly
wondering, is the time coming to let you fly in a new way? I truly
desire you to fly fully. I know you are so much bigger than what
it appears right now. I can feel it. I see your brand and product
everywhere. I think I need some help with all this. I know you've
got me. Thank you for being up to such incredible things. I'll stay
present with you. Each moment of each day. I'll bask in this time
with you. Thank you for choosing me. I love you.

* * *

KAKAO,
Thank you for being here with me, guarding me, inviting me to fly
and showing me the beauty, the playground, the peace, the music, the
dance of it all. The freedom, the play, the ease, the timelessness, the
openness, the love. Thank you for connecting to me in this lifetime,
thank you for choosing me to dance with, to deliver your message,
wisdom and beauty through. Thank you for teaching me. May I be
a pure channel for you to come through. May I be the perfect divine
example for you and your message. Your message that we are co-
creators, that we are free to fly wide and high, that when we choose
to, we experience our divine birth rights of freedom, abundance,
goddess-ness, beauty, intimacy, fun, lightness. You are so gorgeous,
you move me greatly, your invitation is intoxicating. You teach me
so much and I desire to go further and higher with you. I desire to
see what you see, feel what you feel, express how you express. In
perfect, unwavering peace. Unbelievably present, without a single
worry of what's before you or ahead of you. Completely taking in

every ounce of your flight, the wind, the flow, the sights, the divine lift you have provided. Floating in orgasmic bliss, delighting in the movement and playfulness of it all, embracing the pure mystery of the whole experience. I feel you preparing me. And I am so ready to step into you, to wear your skin all day every day. Thank you for the gift of this moment, to fully feel you and hear you. I can see and feel you right next to me. I trust you to take me exactly where we need to go. I ask you to take me there now. I know the journey encompasses perfect timing. My eyes are open, receiving your intuitive guidance. Guide me to the places and people that perfectly align with the foresight, vision and heart of your spirit. I fully tap into the visual expression, to the logistics, to the beings involved that align with your purpose. I am open, ready, aligned with you, committed, curious, I am a hell yes to you and this important calling.

* * *

Dear Delighted By,
Hey baby girl. You killed it yesterday. You absolutely killed it, just as you have been doing so since inception. You have literally shaped me into the human I want to be and you continue to do so. The team you have put together is just insanely amazing, and I know you continue to do so. You are expanding right now with ease and grace, which is a beautiful example to me. You are quiet, yet so fierce and so powerful. Today I sit in gratitude for you. To experience you in this lifetime is literally the most awe-inspiring, humbling experience to date. Thank you for choosing me, entrusting me, and for all these fun experiences that came along with it. I fully allow you to go where you want to go; I fully allow you to channel your intention and presence through me. I fully step into the light and power that you require and deserve. I am at your service, and I can feel you being at mine. Thank you, beautiful. You are so freaking beautiful. Truly, I am Delighted By you. Connecting with you is

such a blessing. I move and roar for you, always and forever. At your guidance today.

Q&A

Q: I can hear the guidance of my entity quite well, but sometimes my entity asks me to do things that aren't practical for my life. It feels like my entity is asking me to take some pretty big risks, but I have bills to pay and a family to take care of. Thoughts?

A: Entities understand that the collective of humans could really work on their trust stories. They invite us into deeper levels of trust, and they like to utilize our money stories to fast-track our growth in this area. Remember that anything is possible. If you put your heart and mind to it, it will happen. A lot of times, an entity will ask you to take the risk—and when you do, the miracle of abundance or support will be waiting for you on the other side. More on this in Chapter 12.

Q: Sometimes I feel pressure like I have to do it all on my own, and I am getting really overwhelmed. What should I do?

A: In the next level of conscious enterprise, the entrepreneur knows when to ask for help and does so right away. The old way of business where the entrepreneur wears a zillion different hats, is dying. Talk to your entity and inquire about what steps you should take so that you can be guided to the right support (visible and invisible).

Q: My entity is so big that it's often very scary for me. How can I learn to trust it more?

A: It is in your spiritual practice that you will learn to truly trust. When you connect with your Higher Self, God/Universe/Source, Mother Nature, and all of your spirit guides, your nervous system starts adjusting to higher levels of light and trust so that you can take the jump when your entity asks you to. In the book *Medical Medium* by Anthony William, there is an entire chapter dedicated to Angels and how to talk to them. This is just one perspective of course, however, I personally loved reading and applying this wisdom. The Angel of Faith is one specifically you can call on, out loud, with your intention of leaning into trust and having faith.

Q: I have so many ideas and directions I could go. Am I unfocused?

A: Set your intention each morning and tap into how you desire to feel. Do you desire to feel focused, clear, and tapped in? Then set the intention—write it down—and it will unfold. Every artist is different, though, so respect what kind of artist you are. Some paintings are all over the place, and some seem more calm. So, trust your own art and what you are guided to. But if something isn't working for you or feeling in your highest alignment, set an intention to change it. One of my favorite centering practices is to imagine closing out all of my "tabs" energetically. Literally imagine the tabs of your computer closing out, and any scattered energy leaving your field. Let it all go. Imagine your body coming into a column of light, which is then inside of a bubble of light that is spacious, clean and clear. Later in this book, I give more practices on how to work ceremonially and cultivate divine focus.

Q: Do you go to DB for everything/every bit of direction?

A: I do not go to my entity for everything; I have a relationship with many spiritual aspects of myself—my Soul, God/Universe/Source, Mother Earth, my spirit guides and other entities of mine. In the beginning of Delighted By, I went to her a lot more than my other guidance systems because we were building the relationship. I was getting to know her voice and how to decipher her.

Q: I am interacting with an entity and I want to start bringing it to life full-time; but I have a standard 9–5 job. What should I do?

A: Only you can answer what is in highest alignment for you because I believe that every entity is different in terms of what it requires in the beginning. With Delighted By, I was guided to purchase a small number of items on a credit card so that I could get started in farmers' markets and work full time for DB from Day 1. I wanted to tell Delighted By and the Universe that I was a *full yes*. I quit my contracted side-work and started DB on my credit cards so that I could *work* the business during the day (i.e. sell my product at farmers' markets and events) and *grow* the business during my nights (i.e. research, strategizing, educating myself on the food industry, networking and much more). I was in my *knowing* that it was going to work out and be big, so I didn't worry about some small credit card debt that is temporary anyway. Plus, I was able to monetize DB in the first week of business by going to farmers' markets, selling as much dessert hummus as possible and also being very resourceful throughout this time. I can't stress enough how different each business and entrepreneur is, which is why it truly is a case by case basis on whether they should still have part- or full-time income streams while working on their startup. When I began developing my juice bar concept in 2012, I was bartending and teaching pilates at nights and weekends *and* working on my venture during my days. I did this for two years, working around 40 hours a week and *also* working full-time on my business venture. I clearly didn't have a family to take care of at the time, and I definitely sacrificed my social life, but that was aligned for me. My plan was to continue to work these side gigs until the juice bar was actually up and running and therefore bringing in an income. In another scenario, an entrepreneur may be working on a tech startup that won't be able to be monetized for five or more years, but in their case, they most likely have raised a decent amount of money to fund their salary and the startup overhead. I personally feel that most investors are indeed looking for your full-time energy investment in your business, or at least that you have an intention of going in full-time very soon (i.e. once you secure funding or get to your business's launch date). I believe it is necessary for every entrepreneur to have a healthy amount of "delusion," or in other words, extreme belief that their venture is going to be successful. I believed that my business would unfold in miraculous ways. Because believing in miracles isn't actually delusional—it's wisdom. Was I a bit scared? For sure. But I was committed to following and trusting my guidance. You should see how many journals I filled with affirmations. So, you choose—how bad do you want this, how much do you believe in it, and what do you really desire? There *are* ways to connect with streams of income whether it be investment, a loan from a family member, or a side gig that doesn't take as much of your time.

Q: How do you visualize, dream big, and receive downloads?

A: I make space for it. I slow down, get rid of all distractions and busyness and start listening. It's in spaciousness and in my listening that I receive downloads and visualize. My daily cup of cacao drops me right into my heart space, assists me in aligning with my highest intentions for the day ahead, and helps me co-create with my higher self. And in the past when I was sitting with Ayahuasca, those ceremonies were next level, full-circle; an out of this world experience that connects me with my entities, my Soul, Mother Earth and my purpose in this lifetime. But you don't need plant medicines to do this! I meditate, go out in nature, write, be in water, and listen to spiritual mentors. These are just a few tools that help me access my visionary-self and divine channel. But I never force it, I simply let it happen, that's the key. Visions cannot be forced, they must *fall on you,* which is why making the space for them to fall on you is a necessary part of the equation.

Q: Do you have a mentor and/or do you believe that having a mentor is beneficial?

A: Absolutely, as long as that mentor is in alignment with these principles of conscious business and are rooted in love and Truth. My first "mentor" was a master plant-medicine. For me, Madre Ayahuasca brought forward clean and unconditional loving guidance without an ounce of human-ness (other than my own psyche, which is a whole other topic and something to definitely be aware of if you choose to sit with plant medicines). She is a fierce, relentless, no-bullshit kind of mentor, but that's how I like it. Her intelligence is infinite, and I have her to thank for much of what I have learned.

I have human mentors too and am forever grateful to them. I believe in investing in aligned mentors. Yes, paying for them. My mentors stretch me, challenge me, and always bring me to my Soul's truth. In relation to business, they help me channel Delighted By and my other entities when I'm not clear on something—I love these "checks and balances" and am delighted by the collective effort in bringing these creations forward. It's important to know when to engage with mentors and when to not. My suggestion is to take it in waves, so that you are always developing *your own* intuition rather than relying too much on someone else's.

Remember that with any type of mentor, the actual implementation and integration of the wisdom into your life is the most important part. Embodiment is key, which is why I always say that life is the true ceremony. So, if you get out of an amazing channeled mentoring session or vision quest, the ceremony actually starts right then. *After* it's over. I have always taken it very seriously to embody the wisdom and implement it into my life right away, in a way that sticks.

Chapter 4

Abundance Codes from the Mother

T he content ahead comes with a warning sign. Do not proceed unless you are 100% committed to circulating resources consciously, being led entirely by your heart when doing so. These paragraphs contain what I call Abundance Codes, and they are only available to those who wouldn't even *contemplate* financial gain at the sacrifice of others or of our precious Earth. These Abundance Codes are incredibly sacred, just as our planet is, and just as humanity is. While I speak later in the book about primal fear and the energy of greed, this entire chapter is dedicated to upgrading your receptivity to money and abundance in your life so that you can thrive. Because after all, you absolutely deserve to. Please know that as I speak these codes into your cells, their embodiment requires the ridding of your own primal fears and a complete opening of your heart that resides in generosity, oneness, service and honesty.

Over the course of the last few years, I have learned so much about money—and I learned it all from Mother Earth herself. My belief is that money and the general flow of resources indeed comes from Mother Earth. Most of the messages I share here came to me in my Ayahuasca ceremonies, but I bet if you lay under a tree for long enough, Gaia can confirm for you how real and potent these messages are. These messages, or codes, have now been engrained into my cells. It wasn't just one ceremony that made me change my money story. In the past, I had written love letters to money and at least tried to create a more loving relationship with it. But nothing truly changed until I acknowledged that the resources come from Gaia and that she's totally got my back. I invited her in to actually upgrade my cells when I had doubts. She is here to not only provide the resources, but to help us change our brain chemistry and belief systems so that we can be in the actual experience of prosperity. No matter how much money someone has—if they are still worrying about money all the time, what's the point?

For most people reading this book, things have always worked out for them, yet they still allow their nervous systems to get tapped by constantly worrying about how they're going to pay the bills and how money is going to come in. The way we are operating from a vibrational standpoint when it comes to money is so important. This vibrational shift is what the medicines and other tools helped me with *over time.* You too can start doing this for yourself now.

Allow the codes below to sink deeply into your cells because they were meant for you to remember all along.

We have been conditioned to believe that money is *earned.* The problem with this is that it makes us believe we have to *do something* in order to deserve money. But abundance is our absolute birthright.

It is your birthright to be provided for during your time on Earth. It is everyone's birthright! And this is what we light-workers are striving for—a more balanced world where the essential birthright of being provided for is restored for all. If you look to nature, you will always be shown everything you need to know about abundance and prosperity. There is an inherent trusting, balanced and interconnected system at play. We humans could do a lot better job at surrendering to the flow of the natural world.

Because of what has been done to our planet, and because of what is still happening through those that are rooted in greed and self-preservation, light-workers have become terrified of money. We have become terrified of contributing to the problem, but in that we have limited ourselves. We have kept ourselves from stepping into our true abundant nature out of fear that a) it would end up getting taken away, b) that we are playing into a system that is not rooted in love, and/or c) that by receiving, we are somehow taking from others that are less privileged than us. We have also believed that in order to really be of service, we need to somehow sacrifice ourselves and be a martyr. Ultimately it is our sense of worthiness—or unworthiness, rather—that impacts our belief systems around money.

The reality is that we are living in a physical, material world. Despite our connection to the light and to our higher chakras, it's time to root down into our reality here on Earth, meaning it is essential that we have a healthy, balanced and abundant relationship with money. It's essential to shift our limiting beliefs and ancestral wounding into a childlike wonder, curiosity and play when it comes to interacting with the material world. By no means do I mean you should become materialistic. I am saying that you should have a healthy relationship with what you authentically desire materially for yourself and own the fact that you deserve it.

One of the first messages about money that I received in a ceremony landed at the perfect time and completely changed my life circumstances (for instance, I called in a new investor within 24 hours of the ceremony). I was in a period of my business where I was genuinely doubting whether it was all going to work out. I was so strapped for cash that I couldn't sign up for trade shows or really get my now-scaled product to the market. In my ceremony, Gaia came to me and said, *Dear child, I am using you... don't you think I would provide for you?*

She reminded me that through my work with DB, she is using me to spread my glitter and light on this planet. She said that my soul signed up for this mission, and that she chose me to be of service in this way. She said I came to this planet to serve her, so why would she not provide for me? Of course she is going to provide. Of course the resources are going to flow in. Of course it is going to work out. This brought my body, heart and mind into such a sense of peace and trust. Ahhhh did that feel so good, so loving, so reassuring.

This truthful message invited me on a cellular level into trusting my Divine Mother to provide for me. Mother Earth desires to honor us, to honor our Souls for choosing this powerful work of service.

Think right now of the ways that you are being of service to the planet and to humanity. This can look so different from person to person. It could look like being a parent, creating art, serving a high-vibe business, doing your internal healing work, being a healer for others, praying for humanity, caring for a loved one, having a heart-to-heart with your friend, expressing kindness and compassion to everyone you come in contact with, or laughing so hard that the entire vibration of the planet lifts in that moment. Think of all the big and little ways that you are of service throughout your days. Write them down.

Now turn to yourself and give yourself a big hug and say *thank you for being of service to the world.*

Go outside, lay on the Earth, and have Mother Nature chat to you about your service and how she desires to compensate you for that. Talk to her about money and the concept of abundance. Talk to her self-worth and what she has to say about your worthiness. Allow her to whisper truths into your heart.

I have had so many conversations with her that by now I just know and live by the fact that my life is of service. My BE-ing is my service. And through my being, does inspired action emerge? Absolutely. Through my being, does rest and deep healing emerge? Yes. Through my being, does play, fun and connection emerge? Yep. My being is my service to the world, and in that, I will be provided for. Period.

I am so fed up with the patriarchal model of earning money. This model is outdated and also one of extreme control. It is rooted in survival and self-service. You do not need to frantically do, do, do to make money and therefore prove your worthiness to the world. You do not need to "work hard" as per society's standards just because you were taught you should. You do not need to force yourself into doing something for a paycheck that is just not natural for you right now.

Let's jump back to a conversation I had with my Beloved, Michael, when we first got into a relationship. He had been doing work that was *not* aligned for him, so coming into our relationship very much highlighted this and he was invited to quit *all of it*. As his partner and in my feminine wisdom, I could feel how aligned this was for him. But him? Oh boy, did he doubt it. All the programming came in—"the man of the household needs to make the money." And beyond just desiring to provide for both of us, he was genuinely confronted by being willing to receive support and resources from anyone other than his own paychecks. He came to me and expressed his discomfort around this and the fact that he had no idea what he was meant to do, not only for an income, but for his life's purpose.

"Babe, where do you think money comes from?" I said.

"Hmm. By providing something of value to someone and they pay for it in exchange." said Michael.

"Wrong." I said.

"From God?" He asks.

"Yes. But you don't need to prove your value to God. *You* are your inherent value, and God knows that. In this moment, you have not discovered your life's mission yet and what you are meant to *do*, so rather than stressing out about wanting to make an income, why don't you sit and wait to be *genuinely inspired* to something? You need to give yourself time and rest, which you have never done before, and I have no doubt that in time you will discover not only yourself but also your true calling."

"I know it's uncomfortable to be provided for right now, but everything is more than fine. Look around you, everything is taken care of. You have a roof over your head, organic food on the table, unlimited KAKAO, and so much more. Let yourself *receive* right now, because your being and your presence is of more service to me and our community than you even know."

"And to be clear, it is not *me* that is providing for you during this time. It is Gaia. She is paying you to calm your nervous system for the first time in your life. She is paying you to be in your full presence. She is paying you to support me emotionally and energetically. She is paying you to sit still, to listen, to heal, to feel. In that space, you will receive your next steps."

I went on to reassure Michael that of course he would be receiving money through his own channel again in exchange for his service to the world, but it would be the service he *came here for*. It would be his higher calling, his dharma.

While Michael's situation is very unique, the lesson can be applied to all of us. True prosperity comes from following your higher calling, which depending on the phase of life you are in, could look like sitting and healing, or could look like publishing a book. That's what Michael is doing now, by the way. He took my advice to heart that day and applied it to his life wholeheartedly. He sat in cacao ceremony every single day—being, listening, feeling, attuning to his true self. At one point he was called on by the spirit of cacao to serve KAKAO in a greater way. All of a sudden, I had a pretty badass business partner! He was finding ways we could manufacturer our product, making cacao with every ounce of energy he had, and co-leading ceremonies for our community. And not just that, he healed. He healed his past heartbreaks, his trauma and wounding around sex, and his relationship to the feminine. He wrote pages and pages to Spirit, he got insanely curious about his life and his purpose, and he surrendered to his greater calling. In a very natural way, he began speaking out about pornography addiction, the masculine wounding around sex, and how to release sexual shame and trauma. He became known in our community for his wisdom on sacred sexuality. Next thing you know, he was writing a book. Actually, as I write this, he is over in the next room in a deep editing process with his editor and publisher. His book *Everything You Never Learned about Sex* is expected to launch in the fall of 2020 through Changemakers Books.

Thank goodness he quit those jobs. Thank goodness he listened to his true guidance. Thank goodness he didn't act too soon before genuine inspiration hit. Thank goodness he didn't distract himself and that he actually sat still when the Divine was asking him to sit still. And thank goodness he changed his relationship and beliefs around money so that he could receive support as he stepped into his *true* life's calling.

You know, there is nothing wrong with asking for help. I had to learn very quickly that asking for help and support throughout my entrepreneurial journey isn't only helpful, but entirely necessary. Remember, I was only able to bring my business to full life because of the financial backing of many others along the way. I was offered many couches and beds to sleep in. Many, many meals were bought for me. I was offered lines of credit in times of need. Not because I am lucky, or because I won the genetic lottery and have some magnetic ability to get people to donate to my cause. But simply because *I asked.*

When Gaia told me that she is using me and therefore would always provide for me, she did ask me to meet her halfway, though. She said, "But you need to tell people what you are up to! And ask for what you need!"

Honestly, sharing with people what I was up to made me nervous. And asking for any type of support, especially in the form of money, was super uncomfortable for me.

She showed me how timid I had been around sharing my incredible vision with the world. I was nervous that if I shared, someone could give negative feedback. Or that if I asked for investment, they could say no. I had been trying to protect my heart from rejection and potential judgment from others.

I implemented her advice immediately, which went really well for me. I share this entire story in the next chapter. In the meantime, start sitting with where you could share your vision with others with more vigor, excitement, and childlike wonder. Where could you reveal your dream, your work, your creation with others more? Even if you aren't in need of money, their energetic support and love towards your mission is a great thing to have on your side. Plus, when you make you and your offerings visible, people know what to go to you for!

The next message I received about abundance came at a time when I was feeling like my business venture required way more money than could even be possible to receive. My mind had not yet expanded to know just how much money was out there to indeed support my vision coming to life. I saw the numbers and knew how much it was going to take yet had no idea how it was going to happen.

In this ceremony, after learning to fully breathe with my entire being, visions of the rainforest and waterfalls started flooding in. Aya was offering me my next money lesson: "There is an endless flow of resources." There is an *endless* flow. Aya kept emphasizing the word *endless*. Just like Mother Earth—the waterfalls, the rain, the flow—it's her and it's endless.

What this ceremony instilled in me was the expansion of my mind and heart to receiving more, not from a place of greed or materialism, but from a place of simple abundance. The vision of the pouring waters and luscious trees began opening me to the ability to actually *receive* resources.

I know that others on this planet are irresponsibly taking from Earth's lands and taking advantage of other humans for personal gain. This book is not for those people. This book is for you and I. Us light-workers should not be limiting our ability to experience prosperity in our own lives. When we know of and honor the Earth's generosity and giving nature, we treat her and all resources with respect, resourcefulness, gratitude and reverence.

This message around the endless flow of resources also helped me purge from my body the tendency to hold on to money for a sense of safety and control. While I am all about contributing to a savings account if that is the phase of life you are in, I do not believe we should be so tight with our money from a place of lack. Resourceful and respectful, yes, while also allowing full circulation, in and out, as per your Higher Guidance. Furthermore, the message got me present to the fact that my big visions will absolutely be provided for and that there are no limits to my creative expression.

Personally, I take my financial advice from Gaia and I let my soul lead me in how I circulate resources. Whether it's a big or small expense, I "check in" with my soul and with Gaia on whether or not it is aligned. I also check in with her on how much to charge for my services. Light-workers often sell themselves way too short when determining how much to charge for their products and services. Everyone has their own unique needs and contracts with money, so it would be pointless to list out exactly what I charge for programs, or what my lifestyle looks like. What matters is what it *feels* like. It feels simple, abundant, healthy, high-vibe, spacious, and in complete alignment with my Soul. I take guidance from Mother Earth moment-by-moment, and I am sure to thank her anytime resources come in or go out. I also remember the message of "endless flow" when I do circulate resources out, rather than thinking that by doing so I am "taking away" from another project, charity or personal expense. In this sense, I refrain from being rigid with my finances. Rigidity is just an expression of control, and it blocks us from opening up to infinite abundance.

One of my investors says, "Currency is named currency because it's meant to flow like a current of water." We don't want stagnant water; we want fresh, clean, circulated water. Same with money. We don't want a bunch of stagnant money sitting in our accounts. It's for this reason I try to circulate my clothes out regularly—I don't want to be wearing clothes with the energy and vibration of who I was years ago; it's no longer relevant nor needed. It's the same with money.

When it comes to savings accounts, yes, absolutely place funds in there each month if possible, however, it is important to check in if you are coming from a place of abundance or of fear when it comes to your savings. Many people still have a belief that "one day the money is going to run out" which drives someone (or a corporation) to build large sums of money sitting in a bank account somewhere, or to make investments that actually aren't a match for their soul. If you are trying to save a bunch of money in order to have some sense of freedom in the future, know that you're doing it all wrong. You can and should be living in your absolute freedom and autonomy now. If you're doing what you absolutely love and are using your life force in service to your true soul's mission, then you wouldn't be worried about having "financial freedom" one day. I think many people believe that a large sum of money would rescue them from all their problems. But it can't. I urge every person reading this to drop what the patriarchal society taught us about money, making investments, saving for retirement, solidifying a financial future, and in its place create a new money story that feels good in *your* heart. It doesn't mean you can't have a savings account or save for your future—you can—but don't do it because your father taught you that it was the safe thing to do or because you're incredibly unhappy with your life as it is today. Don't do it from fear or the delusion of having freedom in the future. We are in completely different times now, so can we please create new, fresh ways to approach the circulation of resources? You have the opportunity to be free and aligned *now*, but it'll probably take some more guts than your parents were/are willing to use.

I also feel people use money as a way to maintain some sense of control in their life. They write out their budget, they make sure all the numbers add up, and they worry about the months ahead. They even judge themselves for "spending" too much the month before, thinking "ugh, if only I could have more control and restraint around my spending!" God, what a drain! Our freedom lies in letting go of this control around money, and surrendering to a more relaxed, open, receptive mode with our beautiful Momma Gaia. I am *not* glorifying irresponsible spending here, but instead I am encouraging *more* self-responsibility. To bring intention and thoughtfulness about who and what you circulate resources to is the most responsible thing we could do because it means we are respecting money as sacred and powerful. In fact, I don't say that I spend money, I choose to say, I *invest* money. So, ask yourself great questions every time you go to "invest" your money in something. Do I actually love this? Is this nourishing? Is this a company or person I want to support? Does spirit want to move through me in this way? Am I investing in this from fear or from freedom?

Money is extremely powerful energy, which is why I encourage circulating it and detaching to how much money is sitting in your bank account. I have incredible, conscious accountants and bookkeepers that are on top of the finances of my businesses on the daily. But for me personally, it doesn't work to get caught up in budgeting, lots of spreadsheets for personal expenses, or doing anything that will make me feel limited. If I were to create a budgeting spreadsheet, I would be defining exactly how much is coming in and how much is going out—but that's not what

I want to do. My energetic spreadsheets are full of the *infinity sign* because that keeps me from putting a ceiling on what comes in and what comes out. Instead, I simply surrender to Gaia's beautiful, abundant, intentional plan. This allows the Universe to provide in different ways. It's like when you're listening to Abraham Hicks videos and you hear those stories of people that miraculously get handed a check they weren't expecting or find a diamond ring in the bushes. I personally have miraculous stories about raising capital for my entities; and when it comes to my personal expenses, I connect in with Gaia and say, "Whatever it is that desires to come through me this month, allow it to hit there." Then it does! And when it does, I turn to Michael and acknowledge just how blessed we are.

One time I was on a walk and talking to Gaia about money. I was telling her my desires for the life I want to live (mind you, van life was not a distant memory at that point). You know what she said?

"Baby girl, you can have whatever you want."

I am laughing as I write that because it sounds kind of like that song by T.I. "Whatever You Like." But damn was she integral with her word! Meaning she followed through on that promise. My life continued to expand from there—in relationships, money, creativity and lifestyle.

I didn't doubt her words for a second when she whispered them. I smiled in recognition of that truth because a few weeks before this conversation I had received a message in ceremony about royalty. Despite the fact that it was one of the most uncomfortable ceremonies on a physical level, Gaia had me surrendered no doubt, and in that surrender, I got a very loud and beautiful message: "You are royalty."

What she did in this ceremony was connect me to the one thing that had been missing for me when it comes to money: my sense of worthiness.

I actually got to experience and feel my royalty in this

ceremony. And honestly, my life has never been the same. I have openly received a life that has me pinch myself every single day. All because I started believing I was worthy of it. The cool thing about this is that Gaia showed me first how *she sees me*, before I ever even saw myself. That is what I call Grace, and it's available to you now. Go outside, lay on the Earth, and connect with her. Let her talk to you about your worthiness and how much you actually do deserve the life of your dreams.

You are royalty. Meditate on that. Being a martyr is dead. It's over. The new way—the times we are in now—this service is *not* meant to come at the sacrifice of anything, whether it be your health, your financial situation, your relationships. This time of service does come with a deep commitment, but it can also come with tremendous play, enjoyment and delight. She wants that for us. She wants you to be in the experience of ease, grace, bliss and abundance. What does that look like for you today? Maybe make a list of the things (the people, places, situations, items, etc.) that make you the happiest. You may see that most of the things that genuinely make you the most happy and fulfilled, are things you already have. And take note of the things that you don't currently have in your life. Start asking for them from Gaia and your spiritual source!

One time I heard about the Law of Sufficiency from my friend Aaron and it has stuck with me ever since. It basically says that you will have what you need, when you need it. No more, no less. And believe me, your soul is guiding that ship. While it may feel safer to have a big bank account, you can lean into safety and trust *just as much* if you have a small amount in the bank. As you implement these codes into your life, remember that you will always be provided for with what you truly need, when you need it. If you think you want to head to a $5000 retreat in Bali, but the money doesn't come through in time, it just wasn't meant to be. Trust that. I think sometimes people believe that when they hear these codes and implement them, that they will start making a bunch of money all at one time. No, I'm not pitching some "get rich quick" scheme. In my experience, the ability to hold more money and therefore responsibility was built over time. I cleansed and purged limiting beliefs over time, and I received more money over time. It's similar to the framework concept I discussed in the last chapters. Your foundation of receptivity is being laid and built upon the more you lean into this work. My friend, Caroline, recently led a powerful workshop called *Pranic Healing For Prosperity*. She discussed how our root chakra, the chakra that receives money and offers a sense of stability, expands over time. But it's important to cleanse and empty out anything in that chakra that is keeping the new beliefs from fully getting in and expanding this energy center to hold more money. She offered powerful healing techniques for letting go of the limiting beliefs holding us back, as well as practices that expand the base chakra to receive more money in our lives.

Don't get caught up in the details about where the money will come from or *how* it will flow to you. That isn't the point and it should not be the focus. Our minds are way too limiting to even understand the miracles that can and will come our way when we simply open ourselves up to receiving. Your abundance is not in relation to how many clients you have or how many units of product you sell. It's not in relation to how much money you've raised for your entity. It's not in relation to anything that you do, but rather to your vibration. If you feel that you are worthy, that you deserve to prosper, and are in a space of receptivity (an open heart and open mind), the money *will* flow in a way that is in alignment to your soul and the soul of your business.

The vibration of your being will either tell the Universe that you are a match to receiving the abundance that is your birthright, or it will tell the Universe that you actually don't want money to flow in abundantly. Did you know that you could actually be telling the Universe "no" to money and more resources? If you've heard of the Law of Attraction, then you know what I am referring to. But I want to simplify the Law of Attraction here and speak frankly. Your energetic match to prosperity, love, support and creativity is in direct relation to the *gratitude* that you do or don't embody. The most grateful people I know are also the most financially stable. Is that a coincidence? In my opinion, no. Gratitude is the key to everything, let alone receiving resources. And I don't mean just listing out your top ten gratitudes every day or saying a simple thank you. I am talking about *letting life hit you* and *feeling washed over by the energy of gratitude.* How often do you throw your arms open wide and bask at how blessed you are? How often do you really sit in the energetic field of gratitude, letting all of the blessings in your life penetrate your heart space to the point of tears? How often do you let your heart blossom open and send goosebumps through your entire body at the thought of all the people you love in your life? How often do you give gratitude for all the big things and all the small things in your life? This is now your protocol as a conscious entrepreneur. Embody gratitude on an energetic sense and watch the resources begin to flow.

One of my favorite ways to live in gratitude is to nurture those things, people, places and situations I currently have in my life. In regard to my personal belongings, I take really good care of them. I appreciate them through the way I care for them and keep them clean. I take pride in this! For instance, I go the extra measure to clean our backpacks after we travel, and to even clean our shoes regularly. Michael and I keep our car as clean as possible. It's similar to how I take care of my physical body—I appreciate and respect my sacred temple by nourishing it with high vibe, healthy foods, drinking the best water, protecting myself from Electromagnetic Frequencies (EMFs), getting plenty of fresh air, and moving my body in a way that feels amazing. These efforts contribute to my body's overall health. You can do this with your belongings and your home space and watch your sense of abundance increase immediately. You can do it with the people in your life too—nurturing your relationships and exuding thoughtfulness and generosity is a quick way to feeling more abundant.

Let's address one big issue that surrounds money so that you can be absolutely free and sovereign in your relationship to it. That issue is: shame. I have met many conscious entrepreneurs who carry much shame around their past with money, especially around debt that they may still have. Some feel shameful about the fact that they aren't yet thriving financially in the first place, having been made to feel that if they don't have a lot of money then it must mean they haven't done enough "inner-work" around it. Some are shameful about how much money they made in the past before their awakening, whether it was how they made the money or how they used it. There is shame around money, period. And the reason is because money was initially created from a place of fear, leaving many empathic light-workers to fear money itself, or to associate money with being evil. You are here to help heal this. In *The Gene Keys* by Richard Rudd, he discusses the importance of residing in both the Spiritual and Material worlds in equal balance. I tend to very much agree with him. I encourage entrepreneurs to be grounded in the physical world so that they can have the most impact, which also invites them into healing their fear, resentment, anger, sadness and grief associated with the corrupt systems and powers at hand. If you desire to heal a system, it doesn't mean you need to unplug from it all together. I support the intention for creating alternatives such as cryptocurrency to our corrupt systems, however, I think there is still something missing. In this very moment, my businesses are using the standard bank accounts and finance systems to exchange our resources and in doing so I believe we are infusing love and light into those systems. I don't know if we will use those platforms forever, nor do I know if as a human race we will even need money at all in the future. But in this moment, we do, and in fact there is a lot of good we are doing with that money.

To heal any shame you carry around money means to fully forgive yourself for all of your past decisions, and forgive the collective for theirs. You have done the very best you can with the information you were given—which if you're anything like me, you weren't given a lot. I invite you to wrap love and healing energy around all of your bank accounts, credit cards, loans, and anything else tied to your finances. Send light into all of your accounts and ask for the angels to protect them from anything low-frequency. You can clear and cleanse your accounts often, asking any lower energies to be returned to the light, wrapping your accounts in protection and love, and upgrading them to hold more light.

Core Abundance Codes:

1. Abundance is your birthright.
2. Align to your true calling in life and step into it now.
3. You are being utilized by Gaia, so you must believe she will provide for you.
4. Share your dream and passion with others, make yourself visible, and don't be afraid to ask for support.
5. There is an endless flow of resources, so open yourself up to truly receiving abundance and experiencing prosperity.
6. You are royalty.
7. Gratitude is the key.
8. Take excellent care of what you have.
9. Let money flow, never hanging on too tight.
10. Release all shame and fear associated with money.

When you do this kind of work—raising your vibration, changing your belief systems, aligning your cells with those belief systems, and meditating and intending to go higher for the greater good of all, here is what Gaia thinks to herself: "Fantastic. They are in the receptivity mode; they are ready to be supported; they are ready for me to *catch them;* they are ready for me to take care of *everything* for them; they're ready to get out of the way, let go of control so that I can do everything *through* them. They're ready to enjoy what I am bringing through; they're ready for me to give it all to them so that they don't have to worry and stress all the time." This is what she wants. She just wants you to be in service. She wants you to delight in that experience. She really wants to catch you. She is a representation of our Divine Mother—our original, real, cosmic mother. She has an infinite ability to catch every single one of us at the same exact time. Every time I have a human-as-fuck thought about money or a worry of not having enough, I give it to Her. I say, "Gaia, will you take this fear from me and transform it?" And she does just that. You can release anything into Gaia, and she will transform it into light and love to be sent back out into the Universe. She really does desire to catch us, and money is one of the beautiful ways that bring us back to her. If there wasn't the concept of money, then there would be one less reason to intimately lean into our Mother during this very important time.

Chapter 5

Conscious Capital-Raising

I have come to define what the new way of raising capital means to me through my experiences with Delighted By. I did not go to formal business school, but I have always been an entrepreneur. While I have worked some side jobs such as nannying and bartending at certain parts of my life, I have never had a traditional corporate job or a 9–5. Being an entrepreneur and surrounding myself with business communities since the age of 22 taught me what it means to raise capital in a traditional sense — in the 3D world. I was in a business incubator where I was taught to put together formal pitch decks, financial projections, and learn how to present my business concept(s) to qualified investors. I was taught to base my business decisions on these spreadsheets and projections in order to "minimize risks" and only take "calculated risks." I remember working on Osaka Sun Blendery with this mindset. Honestly it was scary because according to the spreadsheets I was going to have to sell more smoothies than I thought could even be possible in order to cover the projected overhead. I see how some entrepreneurs who go about their business solely with this concept leading, end up halting their idea altogether out of fear and uncertainty.

Considering Delighted By was birthed within 24 hours after my first Ayahuasca ceremony, it obviously had quite a different DNA and was therefore going to be operated from a completely different place financially speaking. I didn't know exactly how at the time, but I just knew that DB was going to be run from a place of guidance, flow, and an energy of allowing as opposed to the more structured and fear-based space I had used to run my previous three businesses. Mind you, I had some success with business in the past and even sold my first business by the age of 25, but I could feel that there was a much bigger, more fulfilling, and *easier* approach that I would align with for DB. Meaning initially no business plans, no made up financial projections, nothing from the *mind*. Just heart, soul, vision and personal alignment every step of the way. I believed this would work. Which is precisely why it did…

The ways that I raised capital for Delighted By are nothing short of miraculous. I began Delighted By in February 2015. After the first month of being in farmers' markets my schedule was packed with attending events, making the product in my kitchen, and trying to scale the business at the same time. I was running every part of the business. A mentor of mine from the incubator I was in, SEEDSPOT, encouraged me to raise some capital and get some help. I had the idea to apply to Shark Tank in my first attempt to raise some seed capital whilst I was driving home after an event.

I applied to Shark Tank online, and they quickly followed up asking me to record a video for the next round of casting. I was asking for $60K in exchange for 20% equity, which would allow me to get to the next stage by hiring some help and hopefully get into a bigger manufacturing facility. I submitted my video to Shark Tank in April 2015 and also emailed it to a select handful of people in my network to gain some energetic support for my application. I was also raising $10K of crowdfunding via KIVA, a platform that offers 0% interest loans, raised from your community and paid back to them over time. In that email to my network, I included a contact of mine named Candice, who I had met through SEEDSPOT and was a business idol of mine in many ways. She's a total badass who helped launch, grow and run the TOM'S Shoes One for One brand. Candice was known for her entrepreneurial and evangelistic spirit, having been involved with many charitable projects. Plus, I had so much personal respect for her, knowing that she had stepped away from the busy-ness and stress of life so that she could take better care of herself and to be a mom. This really resonated with me, and now I sit here realizing just how similar a path we are on, which I definitely didn't even realize at the time.

Candice emailed me back right away and said she would be in town that weekend so would love if I could bring some hummus to her daughter's first birthday party. I was honored she even asked. I brought her eight tubs of hummus with zero expectations other than excitement for her to try the hummus. When I was there, she asked me a lot of questions about DB and the business itself. Then, she invited me downstairs to her office so that she could "write me a check"—which to me meant pay for the hummus. I told her I wanted to give it as a gift anyway. She proceeded to write a check and handed it to me—it said $20,000. I looked up at her in shock and she said she wanted to invest in DB. Both of us crying and hugging, she said to me, "I just want you to know to keep going." She went on to explain that she doesn't need or desire to be super involved because her focus is on being a mother, but that she is here if I need anything. She told me she really believes in me and what I am up to with Delighted By.

I cannot even tell you what it felt like to be driving away from Candice's house with not only funding in hand, but the sweetest soul in the world having just reminded me to keep going. I was in shock, and until this day I am forever grateful to Candice's faith, wisdom and love for me in that moment and every day since then. It brings emotion to me as I write this, reminiscing about the time when all of this was just a dream, yet someone as incredible as Candice saw me and *believed in my dream*. Until this day, Candice has remained a fairly silent investor as she does mom-life in Southern California, yet she is always there when I need her, and her energetic support has been felt strongly every step of the last several years. Some of my favorite advice she ever told me was, "Trust yourself." It has been ringing in my ears ever since she wrote those simple words.

This initial capital-raising moment was simple yet profound for me. I sent Candice an Operating Agreement a couple of weeks later, but the money went to work in the business right away. That same exact week, the crowdfunding campaign of $10K was fully funded and deposited into the DB bank account. So now I had raised $30K of seed capital without a formal business plan—but rather simply a massive heart with a big vision and a unique, viable product that was first to market. But this wasn't just any seed capital, it was *aligned* capital. Dollars that were of high vibration, having come from people with heart-centered intentions and complete trust in me to operate my business in a new, conscious way. Thanks to Candice and her belief in DB, I was able to downsize to a suitcase and get on the road in search for a contract manufacturer who could scale my product. After six months of trial and error, I finally joined forces with a fantastic manufacturer in the Northeast, who I am still with until this day.

In January 2016, I was in a ceremony where Aya told me how important it is that I share with people what I am up to. She showed me how *quiet* I had been about DB, the journey, the vision and she invited me into sharing more with the people with whom I come into contact. She said she wants to provide for DB and for me but telling others what I'm up to is essential for connecting me to the right people.

When you have a business in its early stages, you may not be as outspoken about your vision because it's not "there" yet. In my case, explaining to people what dessert hummus was and that I am setting out to create a new category in the food industry, sounded kind of crazy. Especially because we hadn't made any money or proven the concept at scale yet. Despite how awkward this can be at first, it's essential that you share, with the intention of simply sharing. Request and you will receive— when you tell people what you're up to, support can find you much easier.

Twenty-four hours after hearing this message in ceremony I was being driven to the Phoenix airport when I realized I had forgotten my boots at my friend's house. These boots were my only pair of closed-toe shoes that I owned, and I definitely needed them because I was flying to San Francisco for a Shark Tank casting call right when I landed. I told my friend to turn the car around so I could grab them, which then made me very late for check in. By the time I walked into the airport, I had 37 minutes to get on the plane, and the airport was busier than I had ever seen it. I walked up to the line and asked these very kind people if I could possibly cut in front of them, in hopes that I could still make my boarding time. They said yes (thank you) but right when I hopped in and looked down the line, I knew I wasn't going to make it—way too many people were still in front of me. So, I gave up the idea of making my flight, and thought, *while I stand here in line to re-book the next flight, I might as well connect with these people that let me cut in front of them.* I complimented her yoga pants and found out her name was Jocelyn. She asked if I was having a rough start to the day.

"No, I had just forgotten my only pair of closed-toe shoes because everything I own is right here in this suitcase. I just really needed them, so I took the risk of going back to get them." I said.

"Why is this everything you own?" Jocelyn asked, as she looked down at my one suitcase somewhat confused. Insert Aya in my head saying, *remember when I told you to tell people what you're up to? This is your chance...*

Normally I would brush it off and be shy, but with Aya guiding me, I went into detail. I told Jocelyn about my hummus company called Delighted By and that I am living on the road with the intention of launching my product to shelves... the whole shebang. I told her I was on the way to a Shark Tank casting call because I want to raise my next round of capital to help DB get to the next stage.

"Oh my gosh, that's so cool! My husband and I are actually looking into startup companies to invest in. We should definitely connect more on this." said Jocelyn.

I stood there a bit stunned. In my mind I was quietly thinking, *hmmm this girl looks kind of young, and that would be way too good to be true if she actually was interested in investing in DB.* So, in a way I kind of blew off her comments in my head, but regardless I genuinely loved connecting with her on a personal level so I gave her my contact info. To my surprise, Jocelyn reached out within a couple of days, *totally* following through! We connected on the phone where I shared more of my story, my vision, and what I needed to get there. Jocelyn expressed that she is genuinely interested and will talk to her husband, Aaron, about this more. Within days I was on the phone with both of them. I sent them some hummus (they loved it). Within another week I was on the last phone call with them and Aaron asked me one last question.

"Makenzie, what is driving you?"

"Well, the answer is kind of spiritual, I hope that's okay with you." I responded.

"Of course, that's the only place we live from." said Aaron.

Phew, I thought. What a relief and a bit of disbelief at his response (#pinchme).

I explained to him about my purpose to spread my glitter, to inspire other people to do the same, and that DB is a means to do so.

Aaron expressed how meaningful this answer was to him, and long story short Jocelyn and Aaron were invested in Delighted By within another week. Meaning they transferred the $50,000 into DB's bank account, not because I had an amazing pitch deck or business plan, but because the Freemans and I were an energetic match to sitting at this table we call DB. This is how faith, full expression, sharing my mission, following my guidance, and holding to my unique journey led to calling in aligned investment. And c'mon—now the *three* most high-vibe investors that you could possibly imagine holding energetic space as shareholders in this company!

This investment funded our first trade shows, travel to meetings to help get us through retail doors, and final touches to make our product ready for those shelves. DB's product wasn't even on the shelves when Aaron and Jocelyn invested in DB, but after connecting on the vision and aligning on the product, they were a yes to her and to me. Until this day Jocelyn and Aaron are some of my best friends, and they have truly been the most constant, unconditional support for me on the wild journey. I have shown up to their house month after month to land for a few days or more at a time, considering it the closest thing to home that I knew for a couple of years. We have even gone through hard times together, and yet it always brings us closer. Why? Because of the kind of human beings they are. They always come back to love and they value relationships above all else. Reflecting on this brings tears to my eyes yet again. Ah, *of course* DB chose them as investors. If they can hold the frequency of love and value sacred relationships across the board, then they can certainly hold the frequency for DB.

The story only gets better from here, but I want to pause for a moment and offer some wisdom. Not all money is the same. Believe it or not, *you can be picky about which money you accept into your business.* This applies to investments, it even applies to customers. Get clear on the values of your sacred entity, write them down, and bring a loving discernment into your capital-raising process. Because at the end of the day, your investors are your partners that will be there when shit hits the fan, when you're burnt out, when there is tons to celebrate, and everything in between. Make sure with every ounce of you that your investors can hold the big vision that you carry within your heart, because it is so much more than a financial investment. Your entity is an investment into future generations, into our planet, and into our ascension process.

In the summer of 2016, I was on my way to the Fancy Food in NYC, just one week after we discontinued our Chocolate Chip Hummus from the mold incident. My manufacturer called me to tell me they're putting me on "credit hold" because we owed them $35K from the last batch of product they made. They said that all of my product in the warehouse would be withheld until we paid them—but since we didn't get paid for our recalled product, we were behind on cash flow.

My Aunt Amy and I walked into my Sozie's house (Sozie is my grandmother) in Ohio just a day before the show, and Amy expressed to Soz what was going on. I ran off to the other room because I had some work to do, but by the time I walked back out, Soz and Amy told me they were going to empty out some of their stocks so they could pay the manufacturer and release the credit hold. I was shocked. For one, I had no idea this could even be possible for them to do. And two, this was a bit out of my Sozie's character.

Up until this point, I had been struggling financially throughout my DB journey and my Sozie and Aunt Amy knew I never let this stop me. They had seen me come in and out of that house while living in my van and traveling up and down the east coast. They had experienced my passion, drive and pioneering a new way of bringing a vision to life for the past one and a half years. My Sozie was the biggest cheerleader of me but up until that day I didn't know if she *really* believed it was all going to work out. Amy emphasized to her how necessary it was that we find a solution—and in that moment they totally came to the rescue. They got on the phone with their financial advisor immediately and had the funds to me so that I could pay my manufacturer and get my product released.

As challenging and emotional as that credit hold with my manufacturer was, I would never take it back because now my blood family had invested in Delighted By. It meant the world to me to have my own Sozie and Aunt Amy see enough in DB and me to personally invest in it. It was a true and literal miracle. It's hard to express just how meaningful this huge gesture was to me, because they were the two people closest to me and therefore saw the most. They were privy to the ups and downs, and to my non-stop fire for DB. Therefore, it was so much more than the money to me—it was them showing me it was safe to keep going.

One day after this happened, I was loading up the van for the trade show. As I walk through my Sozie's living room, the CFO of the one of the largest food brands in the country called me. I stopped dead in my tracks. He proceeded to tell me that he had heard about my brand at a trade show, and that at a recent meeting their team was talking about it. He said he wanted to meet me to discuss potentially investing in Delighted By, saying that they were hoping to begin a sort of Incubator and Investing Platform for startup food companies.

At the Fancy Food show, many of the company's executives came into town to meet with me and begin the relationship. We continued discussions at their headquarters and production facility in the following weeks. At the time, we were discussing potential investment as they were looking to be an innovative incubator for startup food brands and believed DB could be a test. There were lawyers involved due to the nature and size of their business, which not to my surprise, dragged the process out quite a bit. The board members of their parent company kept changing the proposed deal, requiring deeper negotiation and conversing. During all the back-and-forth, one of the executives called me and told me that the parent company needed more time to dive into it to be sure it was in alignment for them.

"It's going to take a bit more time and back-and-forth between the lawyers. (Pause) But... you need money now, don't you?" He asked.

I told him he was correct in that. I knew that cash flow was looking tight again and that this next stage was going to require at least $100K.

"Well, what I can do is wire you some money in the meantime, and we can treat it like a consulting fee between you, Makenzie Marzluff, and us, the company. And then, if/when the deal goes through, this will be subtracted from the total investment." He responded.

He seemed very confident and hopeful that we would be coming to a final agreement, and that this was a way to keep DB operating while in conversations. I was definitely a bit skeptical, so I got quiet with my guidance on the whole thing. I heard a, "yes, you're safe, do it."

Within 24 hours they got a contract over, which my lawyers approved, and they wired Delighted By $100,000.

The executive made me promise one thing, however...

"Makenzie, you just have to promise not to live in that van anymore."

He had seen my van parked outside of their headquarters and knew I was living out of it. I think the Dad in him was genuinely worried.

In the end, they proposed a complete acquisition of Delighted By Hummus because the board members of their parent company desired to have 100% of the control if they were going to invest their money. This wasn't in alignment for me. I was not ready to turn DB over—I knew there was more for her and me to do together. So, I walked away from it completely. They never brought up the wire transfer, though. Both sides kept their word. Literally Gaia *came straight through* them to provide for DB in the most miraculous way. It was also a way for this food-giant to circulate resources in a more conscious way, which I feel will continue to happen across the board for businesses that have been operating in the old paradigm for so long.

This $100,000 *donation* from what some would consider a "competitor" in the industry helped us get caught up with inventory, pay our accounting invoices that my lovely CFO, Maria, had extended for the first several months, implemented a small demo program, *and got me out of my van.* I kept my promise to him and didn't sleep another single night in there. It wasn't a hard promise to keep, after all.

Six months later we had made our way into many new grocery stores. I was living in Santa Monica, CA and we were on our way to Expo West, the largest trade show in the world for Natural Food Products. I was talking to Jocelyn on the phone (a DB investor and one of my best friends) and told her we were looking to raise capital again to hire team members and provide marketing support. I mentioned that I had been interacting with the energy of our next investors by writing to them and meditating. When I would do this, I could feel the soul contract that Delighted By had with her investors *long before* the actual meeting occurred. It was one way DB showed me that entities are always fully funded from the day of the birth, but *our* job is to be in vibrational alignment with the resources and with those that desire to invest. Jocelyn said she would hold space for this next stage of fundraising, as she always does.

The next day she called me and said she had been speaking to a couple she is connected to through The Landmark Forum, which for the sake of privacy let's name them Nam and Tal. Nam apparently told Jocelyn that she and her husband, Tal, are looking for places to consciously invest their money. Jocelyn, knowing what I had told her the day before, was guided to share about Delighted By Hummus. Nam expressed genuine interest and asked Jocelyn to set up a call with me.

Two days later, after a long day at Expo West with some team members, I had a video call with Nam and Tal for the first time. In this call, I connected with them by asking about their intention, their driving force in life. I could instantly feel their hearts and soul behind the screen. In this call, they learned about me, my journey, DB's mission, and what we are looking for to fund this next stage. I was clear in the amount and equity exchange, and by the end of the call they looked at each other, looked back at me, and said YES.

Within days, the $300,000 was transferred into Delighted By's bank account. And as always, the Operating Agreement was updated and signed quickly and easily. It all happened this quickly because of the vibrational alignment. I had been working on that alignment by simply writing to my future investors and fully trusting, rather than being in a vibration of worry or rush.

My last story about raising capital also includes Nam and Tal, however, let me share a little more about them before I proceed. Last month at our annual DB team Retreat 2019, Nam and Tal came to meet every team member, sat in cacao ceremony with us, expressed their hearts to each other and to everyone in the circle, and no doubt impacted every person there. Nam and Tal have indeed become some of our best friends and family members in this life, and just like with the Freemans, we have gone through challenging moments and yet always come back to unconditional love with each other. Our relationships continue to deepen, and our soul contract continues to reveal itself as we serve this planet together. Nam and Tal have taught me so much about family, parenthood, union, kindness, generosity, service and humility. They have also had me feel completely supported in all the ups and downs, way beyond just the financial aspect. There is no doubt in my mind that DB, just as she chose Candice, Aaron, Jocelyn, Amy and Sozie with absolute intention, also hand-picked Nam and Tal to embed this new frequency of business into the planet alongside of me. I wish I could use their real names to fully honor who they are and what they mean to me, but for now, Nam and Tal it is.

If you're wondering why I have so many capital-raising stories, it's because I am in the food industry. I never knew it would take *this much funding* to launch a food product to market, and to my initial surprise, I have had dozens of Venture Capitalists compliment us for not needing to raise more! I have seen many food brands raise over $30MM of capital over the lifespan of the business before ever securing an exit.

I suppose the need to raise so much capital for a food venture is because the margins are so tight, so there is less available to allocate to talent, marketing etc. For DB it was even more challenging because our manufacturer had very high production minimums. Every time we ran a batch, they required us to make/ purchase around 9000 units per flavor. But in the beginning, our Purchase Orders from retailers didn't amount to that much, meaning at the end of each month we had a lot of product to donate—and therefore, product we weren't being paid for. For this reason, we could burn through a good amount of cash on a monthly basis, which is why in my opinion we needed to raise the amount we did.

In April 2017, Shark Tank called me. I had applied in the previous two years and didn't make it all the way; but this time they called me to inquire about where DB was business-wise. I gave them the numbers they requested. The first time I applied to Shark Tank (2015) with next to no sales. The second time I applied (2016) we had $70,000 in sales. The third year (2017), they called me, and DB had reached nearly $1MM in sales. Due to the drastic jump in sales, they decided to put me through the grueling process of the last rounds of casting which included hundreds of pages of paperwork, interviews, video presentations, and pitch practices with the producers. Until finally, in June 2017 I walked onto the set of Shark Tank.

It was an incredible and intense experience, knowing it was Delighted By's big premier. Mark Cuban offered me a deal for $600,000 investment while I was in the tank, and I said yes. By the way, when you're in the tank, you can say yes, but this does not mean the deal is closed or finalized; it simply means you can continue the discussions and move into due diligence. Over the course of the two months following the recording date, I was "checking in" with my higher guidance to determine whether or not partnering with Mark Cuban was actually in alignment for DB. It was important to me that Mark and I connected on a personal level, heart-to-heart. I now had the experience of being in partnership with very aligned, heart-centered investors up until this time and I wanted to keep that going.

When meeting with Mark, I asked him what his vision and plan was for Delighted By. I shared with him how important it is to me to lead the way for conscious enterprise, and that Delighted By is a platform in which we do just that. When I was sitting down with Mark, I could feel my Soul yearning for my Divine Feminine intuition to be respected within my business. I emphasized to Mark that the "grind is dead" for me, and that I'm desiring to hire a bigger team so that I can step back even further from the operations of the business. At the time, we were growing quickly and yet I was still the only employee, on the brink of absolute burnout.

Mark is a rad guy with a genuine intention of helping entrepreneurs. Yet it was clear early on that he and I had very different visions for DB. We are both visionaries, and it was evident that our visions were going to clash. I asked myself over and over again, "but is this what Delighted By wants?" Maybe she was calling in Mark's energy, experience, drive and resources to grow her in a way that she actually desires? I was doubting myself because I wanted to be sure that I wasn't putting my own resistance or fears into this decision. When I sat down with her to connect on it all, I heard her say, *Makenzie, I chose you to be my channel for a reason.* I knew then that this was going to be an opportunity to be a voice not only for DB, but for the new paradigm of business as a whole.

One week before meeting with Mark for the last time, there were many events that assisted me with making this incredibly important and tough decision. The whole world wanted me to partner with the badass, billionaire, business mogul of Mark freaking Cuban. But I knew deep down it wasn't right for DB and me, and I was going to have to share that with him.

We drove to Laguna and I vulnerably shared with Mark that I am out to pioneer conscious enterprise in a way that will demand leading from my feminine, and that partnering with him would actually really limit my freedom in doing so. Mark 100% got it and wished me nothing but the best both personally and professionally. He has even picked up his phone to answer a few of my questions since parting ways, which I share because I know for a fact that Mark's heart is definitely in the right place.

In the week before I officially walked away from the deal with Mark Cuban, I had called a meeting with some of my shareholders. I told them how off the whole thing felt in my body, and that I think I am hearing a no. They all validated my experience and decision, ultimately giving me the confidence to drive to Laguna and make the final call. To my complete surprise, Nam and Tal decided fairly quickly to put in the money that Mark Cuban was once going to put in. So now DB not only *did* raise the additional $600,000, she did so from investors that I already knew were very much on the same page as me.

When you say no to things that are not in alignment, what *is* in alignment will fall into place. Always. Oftentimes it takes you making the tough, scary decision first, and then the Universe rewards you with a legitimate miracle—a story like this one that is genuinely hard to believe until you see the proof.

All entities, from the moment of birth, are already completely provided for. The details for how your entity is going to be funded are already written in the stars. Why would the idea of the entity come in and you become so inspired to bring it through, if it wasn't going to be provided for? The fun thing about "the new way of raising capital," is that all you have to do is maintain a vibration of excitement and curiosity about *who* it is that you're going to meet. Who is going to partner with you for your entity? It's already been scripted, but you get to be in the experience of meeting them at just the right time. How exciting is that!

I was speaking to someone recently who said he wanted a solid $5 million in the bank before starting his business. He wanted the security and full funding first before launching a product.

"You know, that may not be your entity's plan." I told him.

I am so glad it turned out the way it did for DB because it connected me to the most beautiful souls. It connected me to the fact that miracles are very, very real. It connected me to the fact that Delighted By is *all heart,* which is even expressed through her shareholders—the ones holding energetic space for the channel of her (me). I believe that DB's investors value the journey and the legacy we are leaving way more than the potential financial upside. Their pure intentions and connection to the big picture takes the pressure off of me and whispers into my soul every day "keep going."

In the new paradigm of business, your investors will ask, "what is your vision?" And, "what is your guidance telling you?" They'll want to fully support that and respect YOU as the channel. They'll know to stay out of the way of that channel and simply be a loving, supportive energy along your journey, versus imposing their own visions and opinions on you. It doesn't mean they won't challenge you sometimes, or ask for clarification, or even get scared. But if/when that does happen, it will be on a foundation of collaborative alignment to the big picture.

My shareholders give me the sense of absolute freedom because they respect the fact that there is a genuine relationship between Delighted By and myself. They don't try to get in there and change things up because they know *they are not the channel*. They know that Gaia came through them to support the entity's birth and flight. They are humans too, of course, so since I am pretty unconventional in my way of operating, I am sure some human doubt comes up for them at times. Yet that doesn't mean they project it onto me. In my boldness, and in following my true guidance for all decisions, I am sure it can certainly at times appear a bit risky—but the difference is that they bring it forward cleanly and they are willing to do their own inner work if they have any human fear come up for them.

You should not have to do anything to raise capital for your business that isn't inspiring and exciting. For me, writing a full business plan for DB felt really limiting and out of integrity of my truth. But if you love it and are super delighted by it, then that's probably what you're being guided to do to connect you with the right investor(s). Maybe a potential investor requests a business plan, so in its place you create an awesome presentation that expresses the facts, the vision and the "plan" as it stands in the moment. Do what feels great, creative and inspiring to you!

I know I need to make a note here about paying yourself. First and foremost, you should be paying yourself as an employee in your business as soon as you are able to, even if your business is a not-for-profit. Secondly, if your business is one that requires a lot of resources and time to bring to market before generating revenue, you should absolutely be including your salary as a line item for capital allocations. If you've been in the business world for a while, you know this. But the spiritual community has a harder time with this one because we are so service-oriented. But no, all of the abundance codes from the previous chapter apply here. In terms of how much to pay yourself, just be reasonable. As a startup, give yourself a startup salary, and it can increase over time as your business grows and as it feels aligned for you and your partners. For my first year in business, my expenses were extremely minimal as I lived on the road most of the time and was able to use what I had and two credit cards to get by while I poured myself into DB 24/7. Around the second year or so when the spreadsheets allowed for it, I began to take a salary of $48K per year, which covered my rent in Santa Monica and other living expenses. My salary increased over time, again as the business grew. I have been responsible with the resources I was entrusted with, without limiting my access to a thriving life in any way. What thriving means to you may be different than what thriving looks like to me, which is okay. And what thriving meant to me four years ago is certainly different than what it means to me today. Four years ago, remember, I was sleeping in a van, on a cooler full of hummus with a very cheap, thin yoga mat as the "mattress." I showered in gyms that had free daily passes and brushed my teeth at Starbucks if I was lucky. I didn't know what first-class even looked like on a plane, and I didn't own a car. But guess what, I felt *great*. I was thriving. Now, my current ideal of a thriving life first and foremost includes connection to my loved ones and to my heart space, as well as the freedom to create beautiful things and interact with Mother Earth's beautiful playground regularly. Materialistically, my ideal of a thriving life includes a spacious and clutter-free home surrounded by nature, clean organic foods, access to essential oils and ceremonial cacao, a sick electric car, my premium water filter, and lie-flat seats when flying internationally. Some could consider my ideal of thriving as simple and modest, while others may consider my ideal of thriving as high-maintenance. Regardless, all I know is that not only do I deserve to thrive, I *must* thrive in order to carry out my mission here. My body must feel nourished, rested, connected and clear in order to serve at the capacity I desire to.

Think really big with your entities. Even if you have a personal brand, you can open yourself up energetically to an investment pool. As a not-for-profit, there are also many fundraising opportunities. No matter what type of business you have, the universe wants to support you so that you too can be living your ideal of a thriving life. There is a lot of money that desires to be circulated — especially now, there is money out there that is stagnant, and it needs to be moved. That's why a lot of people are starting to move money and they don't even know exactly why. Open yourself up to the infinite possibilities.

The vibration of the money that comes to you is absolutely important, especially when giving away equity in your business. And at the same time, there are people that need to circulate resources in order to upgrade the energy of the money itself — and this may be a contract your entity has with some. This type of money is not going to hurt your entity, nor is it going to hurt you. In fact, Gaia is taking that money that may have been created from fear and circulating it through you and your entity as a pure vessel of Love. It is then transformed, which will be the actual energy infused into your product and message. Be open to BE-ing a big, pure channel for transforming the energy of money, while always (of course) trusting your guidance and discernment with who truly deserves a stake in your company and who may not actually be ready for such a responsibility.

I leave you here with some frequently asked questions, as well as a reminder that your capital-raising or funding journey will be entirely unique to you. I can assure you it is one you will absolutely fall in love with.

Q&A

Q: I had to walk away from an investor as well, and now I am looking to get back in the game of raising capital. Any suggestions?

A: Write to your future investors. Tap into the energy, values and characteristics of those that have future contracts with your entities. What do they feel like to you? What does the relationship with them feel like? You get to define it. That's what will get you back into the game. And as always, when you write it all out, end it with "this or better" to ensure you're not limiting yourself in any way. You can of course network and take inspired action to meet people who are looking for investments that match your company, but first and foremost you can energetically align yourself so that your magnetic field increases, and you start drawing an aligned investor into your experience.

Q: How much equity should I give up to an investor?

A: The equity you give to an investor is entirely based on what you and they value your company at. I am going to provide the energetic answer to this question, so if you need to know the technical way of calculating valuation or equity percentages, Google has loads of information. Plus, every industry is different, and every businessperson has an entirely different perspective on how to determine a company's valuation.

Energetically, there is no right or wrong answer to how much equity you should give up. It's essential you ask your higher guidance and your entity on this front. One bit of advice: Do not give equity away out of fear of not being able to find another investor. You need to be a full body yes to who you give equity to and in what amount. I personally have only given away equity in exchange for money, so if an employee whether old or new asks for equity, I say no. The employee-entity relationship is entirely different than the shareholder-entity relationship, and I personally have learned that giving up equity in exchange for services can be a cop-out. I would rather raise capital to hire someone's services, rather than give up equity to someone I have known less than five years and hasn't necessarily gone through the proper initiations for holding humble energetic space for an entity.

Questions I ask when raising capital and choosing the equity percentage to allocate include:

Will this person hold the level of energetic space that my entity deserves?

Does my higher guidance, Gaia and my entity "nod yes" when feeling into a partnership with this person?

Does this valuation and equity amount feel fair and aligned? Am I sacrificing in any way? Am I withholding from a place of fear in any way?

Is this a match for what I'm actually looking for?

Chapter 6

Inner Child Work for the Powerhouse Business Owner

In business and in life we have two beings operating through it all. First, the innocent child inside of us, communicated through aspects of our human body, and second, our badass, bold Self, run by our Soul. Realizing this Truth was and is a key piece for me in navigating intense business situations and moments where fear *could* have run the show but never won because of this awareness.

In this chapter I will discuss communication with what is called your inner child, but maybe not in a way you have heard before—because this time around, I am applying it to business. As I shared in the beginning of this book, I utilized inner child work and mirror therapy in 2014 onward to heal past wounds from my upbringing, and as a means for remembering and protecting the innocence inside of me while navigating through the "adult responsibilities" of life. I believe inner child work and mirror therapy to be a profound way of reprogramming the brain, and I have found it to be one of the key pieces to healthy, thriving, heart-open relationships.

Aside from this, I have also found that my relationship with my inner child—that sweet, precious, innocent youth inside of me—is a game changer for my businesses. When I fully embraced her, I found myself to have more freedom with my entities to take bigger jumps and make bolder moves without completely f*ing my nervous system over. When I fully embraced her by having conversations with her, acknowledging her presence, and loving up on her often, the badass *woman goddess* in me discovered freedom to fully fly, press go, and make decisions from an empowered place of knowing.

When speaking of my inner child, I literally think of a real child. To help give some context, I'll share attributes of the inner children within all of us, along with key examples of why this matters if you want to embody the Visionary side of you.

Attributes of the Inner Child:

1. Pure Innocence.
2. They love to play. In fact, that's all they want to do.
3. They unconditionally love their friends and genuinely love making new friends to play with.
4. They love exploring and adventuring.
5. They love the Earth and all her magic.
6. They are curious.
7. They are 100% in the present and have zero capacity for remembering the past or planning the future.
8. They see beauty in the small things.
9. They love moving their bodies around, with no motive or goal other than playing.
10. Seeing someone in pain can feel scary and confusing.
11. They may kick, scream, run away and/or cry if they feel abandoned, scared or confused.

Knowing that your inner child is a *real child*, there are probably certain decisions and life situations that you wouldn't want to involve them in. Would you ask a real-life child, let's say five years old, to: Quit their well-paying job that seems to bring them food and shelter, and start a business or passion project that isn't guaranteed to provide financially right away?

No. First of all, children don't have jobs, nor should they have to worry about where they will find food and shelter.

When I hear an entrepreneur say they are scared of a bold move or big decision, I remind them that their inner child is most likely the one that is scared, and therefore needs reassurance. Entrepreneurs miss this inner child innocence and without knowing it, let a five-year-old run their business, make decisions, and keep themselves from purely channeling their entity.

Would you ask a five-year-old to let go of/fire an employee?

No. Children love their friends and the minute you tell them they are not allowed to play with their friends anymore, they are going to feel incredibly sad and confused.

This happened to me recently and it completely took me by surprise. I didn't realize that I was putting a massive decision on my inner child, which is why I had so much conflict and struggle in deciding to let one of my employees go. It was my big heart and the innocence of my youth that didn't want to hurt, cause pain, put in financial jeopardy, or reject my friend.

I was in so much conflict that I called on an intuitive friend to guide me through this. I booked a session honestly hoping she would "channel" the answer for me and tell me whether I was or wasn't meant to let go of this particular employee. Instead I was humbled by an invitation to do a bit of inner child work.

It was in this session that I genuinely hugged my younger self for the first time. My Goddess/Mother/Adult/Protector-self kneeled down and embraced my Child/Sweet Innocence/Youth/five-year-old-self. Once I re-established this connection and trust with her, I asked her what *she* wants to do right now. She grabbed me by the hand and walked outside… because all she wanted to do was play. *Of course.* I realized right then and there that I had been putting a huge responsibility on her to make this decision about my employee.

After I released the pressure from her by telling her she can absolutely go play, that her friend is going to be just fine, and that mom will take care of the details, my physical body completely relaxed.

I ended up letting go of the employee the next day and continued to reassure my inner child that everything was going to be okay. My inner child stayed right by my side and hugged me, crying, and I consoled her. Sooner than later she was off playing and delighting in life again, while my Goddess-Self surrendered the decision over to the Divine. I prayed, called on Sprit to be with my employee as this transition unfolded, and I reminded myself many times that I made the right decision for my entity. This is after all, what a mother is meant to do: hold, console, feel, surrender, and rise again.

I often tell my inner child that she can go off and play, so that I can press go on big decisions that ultimately don't weigh her down. As the chosen channels of our entities, we will come to many moments where we must honor the voice of the entity and make big, and at times scary, decisions. Someone has to do it—someone has to serve in this way. Just don't let it be your innocence, or else you may cower from your strength *or* your decisions may carry less grace than they would have otherwise.

As I operate my business, I often ask my inner child how she is feeling. In this case I checked in with her after I let go of DB's employee. She definitely had a cry sesh, because she was genuinely sad about losing a friend. She was sad that one of her friends was going to have to feel that pain. Chatting to her about this and letting her *cry it out, no matter how long it takes*, is how my Goddess-Soul Self *honors my body.*

I have had some crazy shit happen with my entities, many

of which I do not share here because I don't want the energy of those situations in this book. But I am sure if you have read any books by well-known entrepreneurs such as Mark Cuban, Richard Branson or Lorna Jane, you know that when it comes to business, the unthinkable can happen. While it may seem grueling and confusing at the time, this is the brilliance of our entities as they guide us—their human channels—for the greater good. This is how they set the foundation they really need in order to leave a pure legacy.

You may be asked to terminate business relationships. Your best friend may betray you in a business deal. Someone may steal your ideas. No matter what crazy shit goes down in your businesses, it is your responsibility to remind your inner child that you are safe, held and supported. It is your responsibility to lovingly let your body release all emotions that these situations bring up, so that you can move on in a more empowered place in your own timing.

In the midst of confusing and conflicting situations, remember your Inner Child. When your entity is asking you to make a crazy bold decision (they often do), remember your Inner Child. When you're raising capital, implementing new changes, or simply celebrating a win, remember your Inner Child. Remember them by tuning into how they feel, by giving them a space to fully express, by loving on them with your affirming words and nurturing hugs, and most of all, by letting them *just play.*

The benefits of regularly nurturing the relationship with your Inner Child are great. You will:

- Reprogram the brain by creating new neurological pathways—this naturally occurs when you speak to your "inner child" with love, compassion, nurturing and calm energy.
- Honor the body through emotional release and clearing.
- Protect the collective innocence.

- Lead your business from a truly empowered, confident place.
- Overcome fear and move through resistance with more ease and grace.
- Become the clearest channel possible by releasing all emotion and energetic blocks that may be keeping you from absolute freedom, clarity and breath.
- Be a badass entity channeler that can truly bring the full visions to life.
- Follow your Higher Guidance even where you're scared shitless or when no one else is supporting you.
- Move through scary and confronting situations without completely being knocked out.
- Have a lighter, more fun, more playful time throughout the journey of bringing your vision to life.

This week I had my beloved Michael McPherson be the guest speaker on our monthly DB Team Meeting. His topic? *Inner Child Work in the Workplace.* I asked him to speak about this because I see employees' inner children get triggered all the time! By me, by each other, by some of the big decisions I have to make, and by the overwhelming food industry all together. Any time you come together with people, especially in a work environment, there is a 99% chance you'll have an opportunity to bond with your inner child. In other words, there is a 99% chance that your inner child will get triggered, depending on your upbringing and your sense of worthiness.

Here is an example. If you grew up in an environment where you were never allowed to speak your voice, then you will probably attract people in your life that make your inner child feel unheard. If you don't address the inner child feelings of being unheard by re-parenting her/him through love, affirmations and permission to cry, then you will probably project your deep feelings of being unheard onto your team members or others in your life.

The only reason I can hold space for the inner children of my employees is because I have learned to hold continuous space for my own inner child. In forming a deep relationship with her and keeping her close at heart when leading my business, I can bring much awareness and compassion to the other people that my business now impacts. This doesn't mean you should make decisions from a place of rescuing people from their own inner child work (I am guilty of this), but rather you'll make decisions from the power-center of your Woman/Man self, with awareness of the inner child healing occurring so that you can continue to pray, hold space, speak with clarity, and live through grace for yourself and those around you.

Chapter 7

Calm the Fuck Down: Purging Anxiety & Stress from Your Business and Working Ceremonially

The majority of the world right in this moment is ramped up on coffee and other stimulants to encourage their productivity and performance throughout their busy days. Anxiety is one of the most prevalent diseases on our planet right now, despite the fact that not many people are talking about it. We are going through our days busy, rushed, and internally stressed. For many humans, they have yet to realize the impact this is having on not only their physical health, but also their relationships *and* their access to true success, creativity, inner fulfillment and prosperity.

I haven't always been perfect in this area. Oh, far from it. I learned how to properly breathe early on in my Delighted By journey, yet the embodiment of that breath came with many tests and moments of contrast. I have gone through phases where I felt completely relaxed and tapped into my business from a calm, guided place. I have also experienced intense waves of anxiety, stress, worry and even panic. I have memories of staying up in the middle of the night, working from the bathroom in hopes to not wake up Michael, while conducting some sort of damage-control for my business or attempting to cross off the million to-dos that built up from wearing so many hats at one time in my business.

I have pushed my body to its absolute limits, overworking, overthinking and ultimately, burning out. The problem is that I wouldn't realize I had reached my limit until I would have an anxiety attack expressed in a not-so-pretty way. The image that comes to mind is my kitchen floor being covered with broken glasses, plates and plants because I had thrown everything within reach against the wall in an absolute panic and overwhelmed nervous system. It was of course around 10:00 p.m., meaning I had been working for 16 hours straight without taking a moment to pause, step outside, or even make myself a meal.

What triggered me into such a state of rage and overwhelm? At the surface, Michael triggered me. He was in bed reading, going about his seemingly chill life, and I was enraged that he had it so easy. I had been sitting there all day, dealing with situations in my business that were very stressful at the time, and I couldn't get a breath. All the while, he is breathing, reading, hell, *going to sleep soon?*

I was bitter and resentful. I felt unsupported, simply because he was on a calm wavelength and I was anything but there. And I felt a complete lack of freedom. I was mad that Michael had freedom and I didn't.

After a lot of soul searching around this event and others like it, I had the humble realization that I had been *doing it all to myself*. I had become a complete victim of my business and of my life circumstances. I had gotten away from my center, feeling like I needed to sacrifice myself for my business. I had no idea that I could establish boundaries with my business. I also didn't know that I needed to value myself more by doing things that would support my body, mental health, and overall wellbeing, whether it's take more breaks, work shorter hours, go outside, cook myself meals in a moment of pause, and exercise. I had phases in DB where I *was* experiencing this balance, but the balance was temporary and often conditional on what was happening within the business. My soul, and that of Delighted By's was asking for a complete upgrade to my personal care routine, and therefore my nervous system.

Those that have been around me personally the last few years know how much of a journey this has indeed been for me. Seeing me on all sides of the spectrum: relaxed and surrendered, all the way to completely zapped over the business that I honestly wanted to get out. I thought that DB was the problem, not me. I have discussed selling my business on many occasions, simply because I was trying to escape her intensity.

Context: According to my *Human Design* profile, I am considered a "Manifestor" type. Human Design is a system rooted in the wisdom of the *I Ching*. While the system is complex, you can find immediate benefit in knowing which of the five simple Human Design "types" you are because it relates to how you best use your energy, especially pertaining to work and career. To find out your type for free, visit www.jovianarchive. com. As a Manifestor, I am meant to create, delegate and then get out of the way. My energy is best used in spontaneous bursts of creativity, and then I am meant to retreat and completely fill my cup before stepping back into the creative zone again. In today's society, this is not really accepted. There is pressure to always be performing, always be doing, always be proving your value in the world one way or another. Learning that I am Manifestor type gave me a huge sigh of relief by helping me understand why I can burn out so easily when I work longer than just a few hours. It also had me understand why I become enraged and anxious when I do things outside of my zone of genius for way too long.

I was acting like a "Generator" type in my business, wearing all the hats in meetings, logistics, sales, management, marketing etc. I took the burden of DB's production challenges, financial dips, employee issues and food industry pressure all into my precious body and felt completely responsible for fixing everything as soon as it arose.

But the role that I had actually been hired for... *Chief Breath-Taker?* I was failing miserably at.

I finally decided to honor myself by hiring the right team and by setting personal boundaries around my work. I decided to honor the Manifestor in me and trust my body's wisdom despite my slight fear of what others would think. I even remember being scared that my investors would judge me for not hustling myself to the bone anymore. My hustle is after all what had Mark Cuban offer me a deal on Shark Tank. In addition to hiring a team and dropping all the tasks that were not my zone of genius, I also decided to change other areas of my life to support my nervous system. I remember telling one of my investors that I had moved to Maui. I was nervous that she would doubt whether this decision was the best move from a business standpoint. But I stayed in my knowing and assured her that my move to Maui has benefited and will only continue to benefit the businesses. The healthier and calmer I am, the better the businesses are. My entities already knew this, but the human in me needed to catch up.

I continue to be given opportunities to embody my role as Chief Breath-Taker in both of my businesses. This title may make it seem like all I am meant to do is walk around and breathe. But no, I am meant to serve in the ways DB and KAKAO ask me to serve, *while* breathing fully. This also means I am *only* meant to do what they ask me to do, not what *my mind* may tell me I need to do. It requires a deep communion with my entities and my soul in order to embody my alignment every day, which is still a practice for me.

Last week I found out that one of my manufacturers had breached our contract by producing a product with the same flavor as ours for another customer. Not only did they breach the contract, but they dodged the issue entirely when I presented it to them, further proving that they do not have good intentions for our business. With absolute clarity, DB told me that our contract is finished, and I need to terminate the business relationship immediately. In the past I would have felt this rush of energy, plus the fear of the future, and potentially gone into anxiety and overwhelm. But this time, I breathed. I trusted myself. I acted and spoke the words I was guided to. I delegated to my team members to help make this decision come to life. I allowed my emotions to arise within a sacred space by journaling, drinking cacao and speaking to my inner child. And I stood tall and calm in my decision, knowing that miracles *always* unfold for us when we make decisions based on our intuition.

These days I finally feel free. Not because things don't go wrong in my businesses anymore. But free because of how I trained myself to handle the intensity. And also free because I have learned to actually respect my true creative role in this business, giving myself all the spaciousness and grace I need to take care of my body and heart every single day while serving at this level.

In your business you will be faced with challenges, it's just a part of life. How you lean into them is up to you, and ultimately is the primary factor in determining how fulfilled and delighted by life you are along the way.

Here is a simple guide on how you can lean into the challenges of your business:

1. Write/speak to your entity to ask the greater question of what really is going on beneath the surface.
2. Give yourself the space and grace to feel it all,

remembering that personal ceremony and self-care is equally as important to your badass action mode. Sit in the discomfort and really *be* with what the challenge brings up for you.

3. Call in support and mentorship, whether it's from your spirit squad and/or other qualified humans.

4. Surrender. Remember that we are not in control and to trust that something higher is working itself out.

5. Listen intently. Remind yourself that there is *no problem here*, but rather something is trying to get your attention and deliver you some wisdom.

6. Act and speak only when you have worked through your fear and calmed completely down in a space of clarity.

Above all, the key to leaning into the challenges of your business is a *calm nervous system.* I named this chapter Calm the Fuck Down because selfishly, I want the world to do just that. Everyone is running around in survival mode and they don't even know it. On a daily basis I run into people that have no idea their nervous systems are overstimulated, yet *I* notice it and feel it in my body now that I have calmed myself down. While I very rarely point this out to those people, I'll use this chapter as a public service announcement to the world that it's time to *calm the fuck down.*

Be really honest with yourself—are you truly calm? Take a note of your inner state right in this moment. Evaluate how you felt today and how you've been operating your life as a whole. If each day you're going from one thing to the next without any pauses, your nervous system is probably overstimulated. If you rushed through lunch today, or worse didn't eat lunch at all, your nervous system is probably overstimulated. If you didn't start your day by honoring your inner state whether with intentional movement, breath-work, meditation or another technology-free practice, your nervous system is most likely... overstimulated.

Overuse of technology is the fastest way to an overstimulated nervous system, with the exception being an overconsumption of coffee. It's no secret that we humans are now severely addicted to our devices, and that our consumption of information, communications and imagery are at an all-time high through social media, fast-paced workdays and media outlets.

In addition to our current overuse of technology, we also still carry an underlying primal fear deep within our genes, which translates to a survival-based mentality around money, proving our worth, competition in the workplace and trying to be superhuman in all areas of our life. So now not only are our nervous systems stimulated by our environment and devices, they are simulated by our internal fears. This translates to unclean action and work without meaning. This completely drains our life force, robbing us of the intimacy with life we came here to experience. Our connection to the Earth, our loved ones and our inner spirit becomes something we will do post-retirement or when we "arrive" to some other place we aren't currently in.

As a sensitive being, your use of technology must be a sovereign one. It is important to know when to stop working, and to also maintain a deep sense of grounded-ness in and out of your business. I stay grounded each day through putting my feet directly on the Earth, taking walks, moving my physical body, doing breath-work, cooking food, and making love to my beloved, to name a few. I have a list of tools that are non-negotiable to me, including:

- Every day, I start with either stretching or moving my body. My favorite exercise is reformer pilates, so I bought one for my home to use multiple times per week. I let my exercise come from an intuitive place, rather than forcing an exertion of energy that isn't there. Every body is different, and I personally prefer gentler forms of exercise. This morning for exercise I put on some really beautiful dance music and got my body flowing throughout the entire living room! If I don't do a full workout, I at the very least do the Five Tibetan Rites. They can be done anywhere and only take five minutes! Look them up on google or read the short book *Ancient Secrets of the Fountain of Youth* by Peter Kelder.

- Before getting on technology, I have a personal ceremony which can include cacao, playing my crystal bowls, picking which oils to diffuse for the day, meditation, going outside, journaling, breath-work and/or drawing a card from a spirit deck.

- I like to write out my intentions for the day, knowing what I am intentionally creating and desiring to feel.

- I put my feet on the earth every single day, and most days of the week spend at *least* one hour in nature i.e. beach, hike, walk, park.

- More times than not, I am in bed by 9:00 p.m. and asleep no later than 10:00 p.m. This means I begin to unwind in the evenings with connection, cooking, reading, self-care practices such as body brushing, or as of lately creative writing. I wake up around 5:00 a.m. or 6:00 a.m. every morning, allowing myself plenty of time for my personal practices before I start anything work related around 9:00 a.m.

My sovereign relationship with technology has developed over time. I personally have gone off Instagram because I feel there are better uses of my time. As someone who is prone to anxiety, it is pertinent for me to maintain balance with my use of technology. This means that sometimes messages go unanswered for a few days, because I like to embody presence in my life. I no longer stress myself out over getting back to everyone and everything right away, and I give myself complete freedom and spaciousness to only engage through technology when my body is in a place to engage.

I have learned the unique needs of my body through trial and error. One of my quirks includes that I cannot have back-to-back calls. I always need *at least* 30 minutes in between meetings. Most days I hold myself to a strict standard of scheduling no more than one big meeting per day. This is what *my* body needs in order to operate my business ceremonially, with a calm nervous system. Play around with what works absolutely best for you and give yourself complete permission to embody it.

To work ceremonially means to treat everything in your business like it's a ceremony—with intention, from the heart, and never rushed. Email is an example I'll use to show you how you can work ceremonially.

Do you answer every email as it comes in, quickly, without much intention, and even at times in a reactive energy?

I have been guilty of doing this many times. In fact, every one of my employees could testify that I have apologized to them at certain times in the business for doing this, now that I have better awareness of myself.

If I get an email and immediately feel some level of stress, responding to the email in that moment is going to *carry the energy of stress.* So, the receiver of the email will feel the stress one way or another. And that doesn't include the fact that whatever I typed in that moment of stress is most likely pretty different than what I would have said *if* I would have paused and come into a calmer place.

Emails can either be *reactive* or *responsive.* The energy of your emails absolutely impacts those that are receiving it, even if it's in a small way, and it certainly impacts your business.

To treat your emails ceremonially can look like setting a container of time aside to thoughtfully respond to emails— sitting down at your computer (not your phone), oil diffuser on, sacred space set, nervous system calm. To treat your emails ceremonially means that you hold an awareness of your inner state as you are typing and communicating. And if you end up sending an email while super frustrated or stressed, which you will because you're human, you can be accountable for it by addressing it with whoever you sent that email to. Tell them that you pressed send too soon, that you could have waited longer before responding, and that you apologize if it impacted them in a negative way. This is conscious leadership.

The energy of *rushing* can also be felt in your business. So don't rush anything. Slow down, listen intently, breathe deeper. As I mentioned earlier, our collective nervous systems are overstimulated, but you get to do something about it by how *you* run your business.

You actually get to contribute to healing the collective's anxiety by taking personal responsibility for your own nervous system — especially in your business. One of the most toxic things you could do in your business is act, speak, write or create from anxiety. So, first and foremost acknowledge that your underlying anxiety is there, and then secondly set an intention to begin purging it from your body and business. I can assure you that you'll get many opportunities to do so. By leaning into the discomfort now you will discover a completely new sense of freedom on the other side.

As a Chief Breath-Taker, I want to remind you that breathing is always the answer. If you're uncomfortable, breathe. If shit is hitting the fan, breathe. If you're feeling anxious, step away and breathe.

Your breath *is* the access to your channel. As soon as you constrict your breathing, you also keep yourself from receiving the wisdom, support or guidance of your entity and invisible helpers.

To start making your way to the freedom of a completely calm nervous system and begin treating your business like the ceremony it deserves, here are some tips:

1. Stop drinking coffee and/or caffeinated tea. You won't know what I am referring to until you stop.

2. If you're guided to replace your coffee with something, you probably know by now that ceremonial-grade cacao is my favorite. It will calm your nervous system, help you come out of your head and into your heart, and ground your physical body. Start in small doses and make sure you are plenty hydrated with water. Herbal tea is great too.

3. Go outside more. Put your feet on the earth and your hands on the trees. Let Gaia work on your physical body. The longer you stay in nature, the more relaxed you will become. Plus, Gaia always has wisdom that will apply to your current life. I always say that at least 45 minutes silent in nature is the fastest way to not only calm down, but access applicable wisdom.

4. Call in aligned healing modalities for your physical body, whether it's massage, reiki, reflexology, breath-work, float tanks, sound therapy, acupuncture, chiropractic, colon hydrotherapy etc. Find what resonates with you and commit to regular sessions. Even when you think you're good, still do it—prevention is key.

5. Use your hands and body more. Paint, draw, cook, massage a loved one, knit. Or for full body activation, dance!

6. Use certified pure therapeutic-grade essential oils in your workspace and throughout your home. Essential oils have completely transformed my anxiety by diffusing them in my spaces, taking internally and applying them topically multiple times a day. I bring them with me everywhere, especially busy places such as stores, airports, and planes.

7. Lastly, bring awareness to your breath in every moment you can. While sending emails, writing a post, driving in

the car, leading a meeting and beyond, just start noticing and then adjusting to deeper, more consistent open breaths.

I now want to speak to the conversation around being a multi-passionate entrepreneur. It is okay to have many passions, interests and projects! If you are letting your soul lead you, you may very well find yourself in the middle of various ventures at any given time. Don't let anyone tell you that's not okay! You get to decide what is in alignment for you, and it comes down to *your* listening of the entities' guidance—not someone else's. Let yourself have many passions, let yourself be ultra-creative, let yourself tap into your full superpowers, while of course always being extremely honest with yourself about what you can handle and what you cannot.

I personally have various projects going at any given time. Here is my current list of things I am pouring my energy towards each week:

- Delighted By
- KAKAO
- KAPU—our App/conscious community
- Writing this book
- Editing and Creating strategy around Michael's book
- Planning an event for our community to gather this year
- Planning our wedding
- Consciously conceiving/calling in a physical child
- Running a 4-week online program
- Hosting a Podcast
- Collaborating on a potential retreat
- Launching a Cacao Ceremony Facilitator Training Program

This doesn't include my personal life, which is full and hearty. In reviewing my phone for today alone, I have had real one-on-one exchanges with 20 people via text, three in WhatsApp, two in KAPU DMs. This doesn't mention my in-person connection time today with my beloved Michael (including our beautiful love-making sesh) and our friend Adam who is in town, the plant-based meals I have cooked, my exercise and personal reflection time, conversing with my team members via phone and email. This is just one day, and I haven't rushed around or felt stressed *once* today.

Here is how I do it! I create what I call "buckets," which I learned from my soul sister Joy in a mentoring call one day. Every part of my life, especially all of my projects are categorized into energetic buckets. I typically have an ongoing list or spreadsheet that organizes my various buckets, which lists out any given tasks or pending items to attend to for each bucket. I choose to consciously go inside of each bucket, and when complete for the day, I close it out energetically. When I am being present with my loved ones, myself or nature (meaning I am not working), if I get pinged with a task or communication, I simply add it to the bucket energetically and return to what is in front of me. When I am back at my desk, I open up the bucket in my mind (or in the spreadsheet) and can reference what the entity is asking of me that day. This practice keeps me ultra-present in life, rather than being in two places at one time, or pretending to listen to someone while having an over-active mind with the entity pinging me about an idea. Now if something doesn't get complete in a day, I put it into the bucket, close my computer, and don't think about it until the next time I open the bucket. So freeing!

I keep my buckets balanced by asking my soul where to invest and pour my time each day. Every area of life requires investment, so I never want to invest all of my time into work and little time into my loved ones. Instead, I embrace a balance now that feels great to my natural feminine being. For me it is all important. I don't pride myself on being a superwoman who can do 17 things at one time, because that is way too much pressure. Instead I pride myself at being good at going in and out of my "buckets" with intention and grace. I love nurturing my body, my family, my team members, *and* my visions/projects. I can't do it all at one time, but I make sure to spread it out evenly throughout the week in a way that fills me up. My ideal allocation of energy continues to evolve as I evolve!

I encourage you to find a groove that feels juicy to you. Find the right organization tools and ways to have healthy boundaries with your entities. There are times where I will even ask my entities to bless me with a little break so that I can rejuvenate myself or have more time with family. You can have a conversation and open dialogue that continues to expand over time so that you don't have an ounce of stress or self-sacrifice running in the background of your beautiful creations.

Chapter 8

Marketing & Sales 101: Get Your Medicine to the People

T he new way of obtaining customers is to create something so high-vibe from a place of pure love and service, that it magnetizes the souls who genuinely will benefit from your product or service. Gone are the days of 3D sales funnels, heady marketing strategies or forcing products and services on people through manipulative tactics. To try to get someone to click a button by using certain language or psychology is a form of manipulation. The new way is to purely channel the high-vibe product, brand and message from a place of service; it's to focus on the *one person* you could impact, rather than getting caught up with how many people you could possibly reach in a short amount of time.

In the new way, you know your entity is sacred and therefore you recognize the beauty of impacting even one person. There are some artists that have left a true legacy of beauty yet never made much money, if any, while they were alive. They focused on their creation with one intention: to create.

We have stepped into a time where we, as the channel, may (and must) focus purely on the "medicine" or "art" itself.

What is your medicine? What is your artistic expression? What product, service, message, healing modality, or brand are you bringing to the people? What impact do you desire to have, whether it's on one person or one million people?

Every product and service carries the vibration that it was birthed and channeled in. Every company has what I call a "DNA." For example, Delighted By was birthed from the heart, with my commitment to being 100% guided by Spirit, my intention of simply spreading my glitter, and my mission to bring a high-vibe product to the world that carries frequencies of love, abundance, compassion and unity-consciousness.

I am driven every day with the knowing inside of me that when people eat my product, whether they know it or not they are pushing a massive love-button for themselves. They are receiving not just a healthy treat that delights their taste buds, but a product that carries a vibration to benefit their own heart and therefore their life.

When we talk about DB and her product to the public, I don't necessarily mention all of the above because that may be a bit over everyone's heads. But as the channel, I just *know* it's the truth, and therefore I see her product as my own kind of *medicine for the people.* I'm lit up by the fact that this high-vibe product I created is literally going into people's bodies, and back into the Earth, ultimately raising the vibration of the planet altogether. I'm lit up that DB is embedding her frequency into the planet. My heart explodes knowing that she is leaving her own kind of legacy that will be here long after I am gone.

My biggest piece of marketing and sales advice: People will feel it. Believe it or not, even the people that aren't attuned to these concepts in this book, can still *feel* the intention and vibration of the fruits of your entity. The people that need your medicine (your product, message, service, brand, etc.) will find it and support it because they can *feel it and therefore will be attracted to it by universal law.* They can feel the intention behind it and above all, in it they can feel the most powerful force in the universe: love.

This is why I tend to despise sales funnels, certain forms of email marketing, all low-vibe advertisement opportunities, most paid PR, and essentially anything that carries an intention of, "let's try to reach X amount of people so that we can translate to X amount of sales." I am a businesswoman, so of course I know there is absolutely a time and place to market one's product. But the intention in doing so really matters and is indeed felt.

Can you feel when someone posts about their offerings on Facebook with a focused intention of solely making money or getting more followers? Absolutely. I know a lot of well-intended people offering beautiful products and services, but you can still feel traces of their lack mentality, their need to reach as many people as possible, and their desire to be "known." There are many entrepreneurs channeling high-vibe entities yet are still letting their human fears get in the way of sharing it in full purity.

While we all are so deserving of being known for, and receiving unlimited abundance for our beautiful offerings, it cannot be the main thing driving our marketing efforts. The sole thing driving all marketing efforts should be the desire to impact a single person in a positive way. For example, when I began Delighted By in farmers' markets, I had one intention: to spread my glitter. I wanted to connect to even a single person and make their day with my presence, my smile, and my delicious high-vibe product. And not surprisingly, the people felt this true intention... and flocked to it. We sold out at every single event, to the point where I kept having to search for new kitchens in which to make my product. When you genuinely care about the *one person* you are impacting, that's when more people come.

The other day we had one single person show up to a KAKAO ceremony. I was so proud of the four of us facilitators in our response. We all said things to each other like, "wow this person must be super ready to receive," and, "oh my gosh, that's magical, I can't wait to see what unfolds," and, "dang this girl is ready for a true cacao initiation." For us, it's not about the numbers or how many people can we reach, it's about honoring the medicine's brilliance in who she brings and when.

Ayahuasca is the grandmother plant of the jungle. She is the single most impactful thing on this planet in my humble opinion. Does she have billboards, fancy websites, marketing affiliates, or flashy packaging? Does she worry about her reviews on Facebook or how many people show up to her ceremonies? No. She calls who she calls. She knows exactly who she is and the power that she has. She knows that those who need to find her, will find her in their own divine timing. People flock to the Amazon to sit with her. Just a single cup of medicine is enough to change someone's life forever, which genuinely creates a ripple effect in the world. No glitz or glam needed.

How could we treat our beautiful, heart-centered enterprises with the same sacredness as Ayahuasca? How can we create something so badass, so next level, so impactful, so excellent that people share about it organically? And if it doesn't go as fast as we'd like, what if we humbly come back to what *is* working, who we already are impacting, and *being* the breath of our company rather than always trying to get to the next level, next sales goal, next big project?

These entities need breath; they need integration time; they need us to slow the f* down and actually receive their medicine for ourselves. They need us to really own our abundance stories, otherwise our human-as-fuck selves will try to promote in order to pay the bills—which is the last place we want to share from, right?

These entities also recognize that they *are* indeed an expression of art. So, every stroke (aka step) deserves articulate attention and commitment to its beauty and perfection. If a painter created a painting as quickly as he possibly could for the mere sake of having it finished, do you think it would be very beautiful? If a sculptor didn't enjoy every second of his creating period, do you think we would admire it in the same way? If a musician raced through his song as fast as possible, do you think it would sound the same as when he plays every note with absolute delight and presence? With paintings, sculptures and music, we can *feel* the state of bliss the artist was in while intentionally expressing. We can *feel* their commitment to the beauty and excellence of each stroke and every note. We can *feel their emotion* through the piece of artwork. Business is no different.

I remember when I owned a pilates studio in Surry Hills, Australia—we were doing incredibly well and people were finding the studio organically. But I was still in my head about it, with thoughts like, "but what about next month?" I would walk up and down Crown Street passing out flyers, completely stressed inside and worried over nothing. I can only imagine how much more I would've enjoyed life if I would have focused on the fact that most of our classes were already full. Or if I would have basked more in the connections with the people already in my studio. I look back and realize just how much I stole my own life force and hijacked such a special time of my life by getting caught up in worry and lack. This impacted my physical body, my relationship, and certainly my vibration. That entity was pure magic (her name was *Glow*) and she indeed magnetized beautiful souls to her. Through her colors, her vibrancy and her spirit, she attracted super kind, gentle, inspiring people that fully received the magic of me. They gave me so much love, and while I did receive it partially back then, I blocked myself from fully receiving it when I'd get into my head.

It was around this time that I was exposed heavily to the old paradigm of marketing and sales. I came into contact with health coaches and practitioners that were still very much ego-focused, and would leverage fancy thought-out copy on their websites, email marketing campaigns and other sly tactics to build their business to X income per month. I don't mean to judge this, but I now have learned a new way to build business from a completely different place that actually feels good to me.

I don't believe in buying followers, or any other action that creates the perception that our business is bigger than it actually is. It just doesn't feel pure to me, which is why I am intuitively guided to support products and brands that have a more conscious approach. I can feel when a brand is genuinely desiring to share their "medicine" versus when a brand is trying to get as big as possible as fast as possible from a place of ego. I don't *only* care that the product is sustainable, made from clean ingredients, or has a bunch of fancy conscious lingo on their packaging, I also care about intuitively feeling into the *real motive behind it.*

It feels fantastic inside to not have to create a perception to people, but rather be real. It feels so good to just own who I am, who my entities are, and what we are offering. It feels good to speak my own language, rather than try to figure out what is going to sound good to everyone else. It feels good to be unfiltered and completely free in the rawness of me. I let my entities speak through me so that our marketing is coming from a more intentional and guided place.

Imagine a business and life where no one feels like you're pushing anything on them. Imagine that you simply create for the sake of creating. Imagine that every conscious marketing effort you embark on is one from true delight and guidance from your entity. You ditch all the things that don't feel good to you and align entirely with what *your* way is. The right people come when they're meant to come, and Gaia provides to you in miraculous ways (as she always does) because you're actually willing to open your mind and receive. Imagine a business and life where you just show up with your medicine. You tell people about it, yes; you share what you're up to and even extend the invitation, but never from a place of force or neediness.

Imagine a business and a life where you are simply being the magic of you, where you spread your glitter, and where you simply brew your medicine and invite people in from a place of service. And in all that beauty, power, pure intention and love, people start coming to your door. One by one, with ease and grace, while you learn, shift, build your relationship with your entity, and provide a renewed foundation every single day for that entity. This is why you can't try to get one million people to sign up for your program right away, because your entity is brilliant enough to know that you're not ready for that yet. Our entities prepare us bit by bit, and when we respect them as medicine, we are able to fully receive what they're trying to give to us every single day.

Delighted By and KAKAO are hands-on proof that this stuff works. We do not participate in marketing efforts unless it feels completely aligned. We never do something because we are "supposed to" or because someone else had success with it. Our main focus is always to put the most incredible, heart-felt energy into the products, in addition to striving for excellence in regard to our quality and integrity. I have found that the more delighted by life and my businesses I can be, the more magic we create and therefore the more miracles we attract. We have been surprised and delighted by hundreds of miracles over the last few years. People have been drawn into my businesses in rather mysterious ways. DB and I were featured on *ABC's Shark Tank* (for free), where all five sharks raved about the product in front of eight million viewers. We were also featured on *LIVE with Kelly, The Today Show,* and hundreds of articles including O Magazine and Cosmopolitan. Social media influencers and food bloggers take initiative to share our product on their platforms, or my absolute favorite—I'll see everyday moms bringing the product to their parties and moms' groups and post it on their FB.

To receive the miracles that can and will occur in this new paradigm, one must completely transform what society has conditioned us to believe about money, making an income, proving ourselves and grinding till we "make it." The truth is that you don't necessarily *need* to pay influencers to post about your product. You don't need to have fancy FB ads. The right people will find you because of a feeling and a magnetic pull. People will share about your product/message, a lot of people may I add, when it's in full integrity with the entity's soul purpose. Of course, at certain stages your entity may guide you into forming strategic partnerships, fun collaborations, and other marketing initiatives that have great impact—but the *come from* is genuine to the soul of the entity. Plus, sometimes less is more to keep the sacred integrity of your circles, your enterprise and your product. I just had a friend share with me that she had two people unsubscribe from her community platform and said that literally overnight the energy of the entire platform changed. It felt so much more spacious, clear and clean. For this reason, I would rather have ten people enjoying our product by aligning with our values as a company, versus one million people simply because we caved in to a bunch of bullshit that didn't feel good to me. I am committed to leaving this planet in a vibration of more love, not fear, so how I go about my marketing and sales efforts matters greatly.

The reality in all of this is that there are thousands of humans who eat DB's product and drink KAKAO, and you better believe how good it feels to know we got here from a place of alignment. These are the kind of companies and entrepreneurs that go down in history for revolutionizing and pioneering powerfully. These are the leaders that get books written about them, because they stayed committed to their own new way. They didn't give in to what others said they should do based on what worked in the past. They aren't limited by the "rules," they create their own rules. Whether it's Taylor Swift, Logic (my favorite rapper), Richard Rudd, or Richard Branson... examples of people who have created pure magic with massive influence all because they were brave enough to believe in the invisible. They were brave enough to not give a shit about the parameters of society, but rather commit to creating what they believe is beautiful. They left (and are still leaving) a legacy because they were simply determined to bring their unique medicine to the world/people.

The wonderful thing about all of this is that in the new paradigm, the aligned businesses *can* be massive. Or at least the perfect size that makes *your* soul truly sing. Just do it—just bring your medicine to the people—and you'll see.

Chapter 9

Marketing & Sales 202: When Your Entity Is Ready to Roar

N ow that we have laid the groundwork in the previous chapter and that you are coming into a more sacred relationship with marketing and sales, let's take it further.

What if your entity comes to you and says it's ready to go bigger? What if she tells you you've been keeping her a bit small, playing a bit too safe? What if she tells you she is ready to light the world up and maybe reach hundreds, thousands, or even millions of people?

That happened to me. After I led my 2019 two-day event in Maui *Restore the Heart into Big and Small Business,* I started receiving marketing downloads that honestly, I was never expecting. Apparently, the marketing codes I offered weren't complete, so both of my entities KAKAO and Delighted By came in to assist the downloads by whispering in my ear and presenting opportunities. It felt like something in the collective had shifted, that the people were ready for more of my medicine and that of DB and KAKAO. They were asking me to let them roar louder. And how were they going to be able to? By *me* giving them permission to roar, releasing all resistance I had to going bigger.

Because I had seen certain marketing efforts led from a place that rubbed me the wrong way, I was scared that I would somehow be sacrificing my integrity if I spoke up and made powerful invitations for more people to receive my medicine. I was scared of going too high or too big in fear of leaving anyone behind. And I was nervous of what people would think of me if I gave voice to how powerful these medicines are. Will they think I'm trying to sell them something? Deep down I knew my truth: I am not trying to sell anyone anything. I very much receive and enjoy my life exactly where it is in this moment. I love the simplicity of it, the freedom, the work and the play. So, if *I* know that I am not trying to sell anyone anything, then I must hold that knowing and detach from what anyone else may think. *Trust yourself,* I heard.

The other fear that came up in this stream of consciousness was the fear that if I let my entities go bigger, the simplicity and freedom of my life could be lost. I was reminded that no matter how large my entities become naturally, the choice to live in simplicity is always up to me. It means I will need to call on more support, more team, and even deeper spiritual practices. But it can still be simple and free. Huh. I was certainly listening. My entities let me address all my fears and then said, "Okay, are you ready to let us fly higher?" I needed to let the reins loose on them because they were ready to impact more people. *My soul* was ready to impact more people. Who would I be to keep us from doing so?

I am an incredibly passionate human being. I believe in the power of my creations whole-heartedly, so they told me to *use this passion* and speak it out into the world even more. They told me to make an invitation to the world to experience this medicine. And that if I don't make the invitation to the people, they may miss out on a huge opportunity to expand!

Could I energetically trust myself enough and hold my stance of power in inviting others towards me, inviting them to drink my medicine? Could I trust the power of my medicine and remember the way it impacts my own heart, making the invitations from this place? I resisted the word "magnetize" for so long because I had seen people use the power of magnetism from a less than whole place. I was now being invited into utilizing magnetism from the knowing that it was coming from my *wholeness.*

I was overcome with certainty and clarity. I am going to be a fierce, passionate voice for my medicines. I am a full yes to inviting anyone who may be ready, and if it turns anyone off, oh well! I am going to share *why* these medicines benefit me so much. I am going to *be* in my belief of their impact and hold strong in my knowing that they can benefit those that I call forward. Those that are meant to engage with my medicines, will, and those that aren't, won't. But you better believe I am going to raise my flag and invite people in with every cell of my being.

As soon as I received the transmission in its entirety and let loose of the reins I once had, the actions flowed naturally. For Delighted By, I hopped on a call with my marketing team and told them at least twenty marketing ideas I had received in meditation. The similarity between all of them? The fact that I was *delighted by* each and every idea. For me, I am not delighted by FB Ads. If you genuinely are, that is absolutely okay! But I am not. I have a long list of marketing and advertising efforts that I am not delighted by, even though they have worked for people in the past. So, my job was and is to find the list of ideas that I *am* delighted by. What excites me? What brings my passion in? What ideas delight me the most? Now when I speak to my entities and ask them how they want to invite people, I write down all the things that answer these questions. I let the ideas fall on me and rather than weighing me down or feeling like a burden, my inspired ideas invigorate me! I get flooded with images and feelings of connection, delight, the human spirit coming alive, and playfulness. Some of the ideas that come through are inexpensive, while others are on the higher end of the budget. The cost does not matter, what matters is simply my delight and enthusiasm! If I am guided to it, the resources will be provided. My entities and I will be entirely supported in our delightful expressions!

I have a few friends with powerful essential oils businesses. They play over on Instagram a lot, because they love it! They are consistently educating people about oils because they are *just that passionate about them.* They invite people into their business and their medicines whenever they are guided to because they truly believe in the power of essential oils and also the power of the business opportunity attached to it. Their belief is genuine, their passion is authentic, and therefore their invitation *feels* aligned with a sense of wholeness. I can actually feel that in these invitations they don't need anything from anyone—not money, friends, connection or validation. They have already gifted those things to themselves, quite honestly. So, their invitation is their way of saying, "Hey, I've got something really cool over here that has transformed my entire life. I care about you and this community, so if you want to play with some of this juiciness and experience the gift it can be in your life, you know who to come to."

Then there is me. I really am not in love with Instagram. Grateful for it, but not in love. My soul is simply not genuinely guided to it, and that is perfect for me! In its place I have found the platforms and modalities in which I feel really great about expressing my passion and invitations. My marketing team over at DB (shout out to my DB unicorns!) plays with what they are delighted by each day, whether it's an email newsletter, fun photography for social media, FB Lives, in-person events, in store tasting demos, or most recently, running around LA in a Unicorn mascot costume. Every month we engage in various marketing efforts, but we only do it if we are delighted by it. I saw a transaction come through yesterday where they paid $1800 to a Costco-associated Instagram account to share our Pumpkin Pie flavor for the fall season. I used to balk at the high prices that influencers on Instagram charge for promoting products, and I honestly used to be completely against it. But this time, I knew that the team was guided, inspired and honestly just wanting to shout from the roof tops how delicious this flavor is. I knew it came from *such* a pure and delighted place, because I know them, and I trust them completely in how they embody DB as a brand. And guess what, it is working! The amount of press our Pumpkin Pie flavor has received this season has nearly trumped the media we received for Shark Tank. We have learned many lessons in what to do and not do in terms of marketing our product, and believe me, this book is not meant to address how to successfully bring a food product to market. But our Pumpkin Pie was a success because a) it is an impeccable product, b) the vibration of the current team, c) excellent execution, and d) inspired marketing efforts that we were delighted by.

Before taking action on any thoughts you have regarding marketing for your business, sit and ask the entity. It may surprise you what they say. When I think about Instagram ads or social media influencers, I think that I am personally a no, but when I ask DB, she sometimes says yes. It's weird but true, so I surrender to it and let her fly in the way she desires.

I sat in meditation two weeks ago and connected in with my entity KAKAO. I knew she was saying she wanted to fly and reach more people, so I asked her how. Specifically, Michael and I were hosting a ceremony here in Maui and we hadn't had any RSVPs yet. So, I was asking how she would like us to promote it. With an open heart and mind willing to receive whatever answer she had, I asked her if she would like us to do FB ads. She said no, pretty quickly. I told my fellow KAKAO-guardian, Aydin, right away and we held to that decision without an ounce of doubt. Within a few days, our ceremony was sold out because our photographer had shared it with her online community of her own accord.

I went to go put together an email campaign for our global KAKAO tribe last week. I felt scattered, burdened, and not excited at all about doing it. I breathed and tuned into KAKAO. She told me honestly that an email campaign is not the best use of my time and energy right now. It doesn't mean I won't be genuinely inspired to it sometime in the future, but in that moment, I listened to my intuition and told my team authentically that it's not flowing because it's not meant to. Around the same time of having the realization, I received an email newsletter from a man named Steve Nobel. Steve Nobel is known in the spiritual community for his YouTube guided meditations and transmissions, which are fantastic by the way. His email newsletter was full of his latest transmissions and upcoming events, a way of extending his gifts into the community and making the invitation to us to engage with those gifts. The email felt so pure, calm and potent. I knew right then I had made the right choice in not sending the KAKAO newsletter. I now had a reminder sitting in my inbox of what it feels like to receive an invitation from a guided, aligned place versus an obligatory place.

Wait to act until it genuinely moves through you. Let your marketing efforts and ways of reaching out to the world come from the fire in your belly and the movement of spirit in your body. I call this *heart marketing,* a term I initially heard of in my work with *The Gene Keys.* When I do post on Instagram or any other platform, it never comes from my head. I don't have to think about what I am going to say. It flows, or better yet it *pours* out from my heart. It feels like an energy coming through my body and out of my fingers, naturally, organically, unforced. I share my emotion, my deep feeling through all my transmissions. My fellow humans connect to the realness of it. I am not saying you should try to be vulnerable merely for the purpose of selling, but I am saying to *actually* be vulnerable. Vulnerability can feel scary at times, especially when speaking about something that is so close to your heart. This is a good thing, and it draws humans together. I sometimes feel that people try to speak about their products and offerings in a way that everyone will understand, but personally I like to be my fullest self—weirdness and all—and attract in those that genuinely bond with me and my message. This is why I don't feel isolated in the least bit. I feel seen, heard, supported and connected to a ride or die tribe both online and offline.

For this same reason, I didn't tailor this book to suit everybody. I let my real, authentic voice shine through. Some people won't get it, but those that do will *really* get it. At the end of the day this is how we can have meaningful and lasting impact.

I wrote this below statement in my journal as an affirmation to myself before finishing the second half of my book. I had put my book on hold for over a year, honestly out of fear that I would have to dilute my message in order to bring it into the world. As I came into my empowerment this past year, I was reminded of how wrong I am. I don't need to dilute my message at all. Thank goodness, because when I hand people cups of medicine why the heck would I dilute it?

This book is meant to serve the spiritual community, or those that at least are willing to start embracing more of their spiritual nature. My gifts, messages and offerings may very well reach beyond the spiritual community, but I refuse to modify my message to serve anyone but who I came here to serve. I will not modify my voice or dim my light to make anyone else feel more comfortable. Some people will get me, some people will not, and that is okay. My goal isn't about directly reaching as many as people as possible, but rather my vision is to reach the hearts that are ready for my message—those that are genuinely needing the encouragement that this message brings. I know that by delivering the living wisdom to those that I came here to speak to, the transmission will ripple out to other communities in a soft, understandable, digestible way. I am here to serve the people who can digest my message now, and I leave it to them and the angels to carry that message onward. I refuse to dim the fire and passion I have for this community. I don't care about being on Oprah or being featured on influencers' podcasts, but rather I care about contributing anything I possibly can to the people whose spirituality is everything to them. I am here to share how I genuinely manage my businesses, which is from my intuition and daily communion with the spirit world. I am here to remind this community that they can thrive monetarily while remaining rooted in their core values; that their guides want to help them bring their vision to life; and that there is so much more going on than what meets the human eye. I bring my medicine, in full potency—not an ounce of dilution needed.

I'd like to use KAKAO yet again as an example of how this works in real life. I believe KAKAO has been an organic success because a) it's KAKAO and b) Michael and I have been real, raw and true every step of the way with our community. We have shared our journey, our ups and downs, our heartbreaks, our celebrations. We share why we are so passionate about cacao/ KAKAO. We share what is motivating us. And most importantly, we don't do any of this with the intention of gaining a customer. We do it, truly, because we are in love with this work and *in love* with the human beings that this medicine calls in. It's our greatest delight and joy, so we share that! Within this all we have formed what we call our soul family, our best of friends that we laugh, cry, mourn, learn and celebrate with. There is no pressure to be a certain way whether online or offline, because they have known who we really are since Day 1. We are safe to be our full selves; they are safe to be theirs. I never tried to do "heart marketing" with KAKAO, but it happened naturally as I allowed my heart to ooze with passion and connection with the people I met along the way. There is a loyalty in the KAKAO tribe that is indescribable.

Richard Rudd, the author of *The Gene Keys*, talks about fractal lines in his Pearl Sequence book. The souls in our fractal line are those that are here to support our work in the world and team up with us energetically on the joint mission. He explains that when one is living in their true genius and sharing it with the world through an open heart, that person's tribe — or fractal line — will begin to attract in as a natural result. He also shares that as you live out your true calling and take leaps of courage into doing so, the souls that are on your fractal line will also make the leaps.

In the sales world, there is a term called "ABC," which means, "always be closing." In other words, always be closing the deal on whatever it is you're selling. Well, I am happy to say I have changed what ABC means to me and therefore all conscious entrepreneurs: *Always Be Connecting.* Take all of your agendas and set them aside and start your trek in the world with the purpose of genuinely, intimately, deeply connecting with the people that magnetize into your field. Be radically authentic, which leads to connection. Clear your money stories so that you bring zero attachment to "closing" and simply delight in the connecting. Share your passion, ultimately leading to connection. And make invitations from a connected, human, caring place. *Always be connecting* is the new "always be closing."

When I feel into my entities, while they both are different, they both have a sense of bigness to them. I receive the image of wings often in my meditations, whether relating to myself, to DB or to KAKAO. I actively lift my wings every day, and I say yes to using them. We all can tap into the wings of a dragon, or even an angel, and let that symbolism lift the energy of ourselves and our entities in order to spread as much glitter as we possibly can while on the planet. The more you know yourself, the more empowered you will become. The more empowered you become, the more you know just how important your medicine is. And the more you know of the importance of your medicine, the more fire you will find in your belly to lift your wings and *fly*. Come fly with me, come roar with me, come wave your flag of Truth. We have got to do this together; it is what we came here for after all. So, let yourself stand in your bigness! Let yourself *shine*. Let yourself claim your mission it its fullness with your song that bellows out of you with grace and passion. Rise up, my dragons, it's time to fly.

Chapter 10

Taking Fear Out of Your Books and
Redefining Finance in Business

I want to kick off this chapter by bringing in two VIPs, Maria and Jennifer. When I met Maria and Jennifer, I was not fully aware of just how instrumental they would be for my businesses and for the way that I view, speak about and lead business altogether. Who are they?

Maria and Jennifer are my bookkeepers who maintain a pulse on the finances of my businesses daily. They also do so much more than the books. They embody the new way of finance and therefore they are leaders in their field and leaders on my team. On many occasions I have referred to Maria as my Chief Financial Officer, which technically speaking isn't what I hired her to be, but truthfully speaking is what she is to me. She advises me and collaborates with Jennifer and me on making all financial decisions in my businesses.

To know finance is no joke. It takes a high level of education and experience to be able to manage a business's finances, but unfortunately most CFOs are operating from fear, which is the foundation for the old paradigm of business. This means there are CFOs and other executives with finance backgrounds advising entrepreneurs, business owners and CEOs across the globe on how to make important decisions in business, all from fear, lack and a survival mentality to ensure that those at the top, stay at the top.

I feel that top-level executives operating from fear could be the single most damaging thing for both a business and to our planet as a whole. The other night I watched a documentary series on Netflix called *Rotten*. This episode was about the corrupt chocolate industry. It showcased the slavery in Africa that is tied to the chocolate industry while also highlighting the billions of dollars that the top three chocolate companies profit each year. The protector and momma bear in me was pretty fired up. In my cacao ceremony the next morning I cried in confusion and despair with the feeling of how we have betrayed our sacred Mother Earth and our own brothers and sisters out of fear and ignorance.

All emotion aside, I own the fact that I have a choice in how this plays out in our future. I carry within me the very power that can make change. But in order to carry that change out, I have to take a hard look at my internal state and biochemical responses to life itself, especially around the topic of money and therefore business.

The corruption and injustice that is happening in this very moment may very well be blamed on corporate greed. I certainly have blamed it before. But truthfully, it's our *genetics* to blame, as Richard Rudd points out in his work of *The Gene Keys*. Humans are wired to think only for ourselves, leaving us in absolute survival mode. Survival mode implies that we as a human species will indeed take down our own kind to give ourselves a better chance of coming out on top. This genetic disposition is why a billion-dollar company keeps it all for themselves, refusing to raise the prices of cocoa by even *one dollar per pound* in order to improve the lives of the farmers that are actually risking their lives to harvest those beans.

If you're anything like me, you can read the above paragraph and feel in your bones just how untrue these behaviors are to our inherent nature as divine beings. What about the human spirit? What about the heart? What about the compassion, love and brilliance lying within us? Exactly. What you're feeling intuitively is the reality that we are meant to *rise above* these primal fears lying within our genes. In fact, a majority of humans have already taken this leap in a holistic sense. But from a business side of things, the majority of the collective is still operating from their primal fear—when it comes to money, we have a long way to go as a species to completely release our fear programming. It's going to take a commitment to learning, practicing and implementing the new paradigm within our businesses consistently until finally, the fear burns away all together.

I have seen first-hand how making decisions solely from one's spreadsheets, versus thoughtfulness of the Whole, can lead to the devastation of communities. The chocolate industry example I used is a massive one. But this happens on a small scale too, with just as much impact on the individuals involved.

My non-profit KAKAO was once approached by a very large company to go about a collaboration that would scale KAKAO's output by at least 100x. This meant more Chuncho (native) Cacao being harvested at above-fair prices, resulting in goodwill rippling through the farmers and community on the ground in Peru. Good for the long-term protection of the Chuncho, good for the farmers, and good for the communities of both businesses. This collaboration required a lot of work both on the ground in Peru and within both of the businesses partnering, and it also required a synergy between two very different ways of operating business. My way ended up getting rejected energetically. What was my way you ask?

1. Absolute transparency between all parties.
2. Commitment to the initial agreements.
3. Heart-centered collaboration.
4. Honesty and up front communication.

All of a sudden, I had found myself within a corporate environment that honestly, I had never been exposed to. I assumed the absolute best—that my voice was wanted and respected, so I used it. I led the project in many ways, doing everything I could to meet a deadline that was given to me especially because I was so excited. I spoke up in meetings when I felt the initial agreements were not being honored. I felt through my emotion and frustration when every department seemed to say something different. And I came back to my heart every day choosing to see the best and to press onward for the greater vision at hand.

Despite the tension between the two very different company cultures, I never in a million years thought this deal could fall through. I felt the potential positive impact of the vision and therefore I held to it. But then we got the phone call. After pouring months into the project and being in Peru for six weeks with our partners on the ground in the harvesting and facility setup, we were told that this project had to be dismissed for financial reasons. That apparently their business had experienced their first "down" year financially, so therefore they must pick and choose which projects and people to let go of until some sort of transition happens. The worse thing is that our partners on the ground had invested hundreds of thousands of dollars into the project on good faith.

We were devastated and shocked, and fearful for the people on the ground who had loans to pay off and had been waiting on the repayment of equipment, labor and more. It turned into a fight over money, quite honestly. We were fighting for our partners to get their money back, and the said company was fighting to keep it. Ultimately, they paid it, but the fight was real, and the impact was great. Relationships were ended which is the worst part of it all. The innocence of pure creativity, collaboration and friendship was tainted all because of a business deal gone bad.

I look at this situation and see where I could have done so much differently. I never should have moved that quickly. I should have built a foundation of trust and long-term partnership with this company before collaborating on such a large scale. We never should have participated until all contracts were signed. And when I felt the mismatch of energies in the beginning, I should have walked away. I had trust in my heart that the people of that company were going to protect my nonprofit and myself personally, so I extended them my hand in faith and hoped for the very best. Despite all the things I could have done differently (and believe me, lesson learned!), I believe that the core reason why this business deal went sour was because of fear. The executives of this company acted from fear. They reviewed the spreadsheets, got scared, and decided to ditch a project that they had already made promises and agreements on. And then from fear, they tried to hang onto money that they quite honestly owed to the ones they signed on to assist with the project in the first place. They had also received backlash from the religious folk within their community when it was announced that KAKAO was collaborating with them. Instead of standing by their decision and standing in unity, they backed down out of fear. After all, if their current customers aren't happy, it may mean a loss of money. I believe that the business, while it may look perfect on the outside, is just like most businesses—it cares most about those at the top. It protects their mansions and cars and vacation homes, all the while threatening the livelihood of a community in a third-world country.

I believe in my heart that everything happens for a reason, and I believe in the human spirit enough that no matter what would have happened, our partners in Peru would have been taken care of by our community one way or another. But this is a principle I am standing for here—the principle of integrity and embodying a completely new way of business that decides from love, not fear. I believe that this principle must be carried by every CFO and executive decision-maker for the future shift of business. And I don't just mean talk the talk, I mean walk the walk.

I bet you that if Maria, Jennifer and I would have been in those seats of power at this said company, we would have chosen differently. We would have looked at the spreadsheets, acknowledged any fear that came up, and held true to our original decision with faith in our hearts and trust in miracles. I believe that if we would have seen any negative feedback pour out from the religious community, we would have invited them with grace into loving all paths and embracing all new members of the community. I know it sounds scary, to trust that one's livelihood isn't going to be threatened, but this is the new way I stand for. Some people could read this and think I am judging how some people make decisions, but that's just not who I am quite honestly. What I am doing, is standing for what's right. After all, that is what I came here to do. I am here to learn and teach a new way of operating business, so guess what, I walk my walk *and* talk my talk.

What I am inviting people into seeing is that they have been making financial decisions from their heads and their genetic fears, versus a new, abundant, heart-centered approach rooted in miracle consciousness. For most finance people reading this, they probably think I am nuts. It all may sound extremely lofty for someone managing nearly $1 billion in assets. But when you do the internal work, it starts to make sense. When you bring this internal shift into your business and decisions, the goodwill that ripples out into your business and other communities is paramount. In the above example, I wholeheartedly believe that if they would have trusted, leaned into the scary decision, slowed down enough to have more vulnerable conversations with me, and really listened with intent to all parties, they would have seen a wave of momentum and success burst through their organization for years to come. And most importantly, the relationships would be deeper, closer, truer. Everyone would have won.

Let's dive into one more story on making decisions from fear. A couple of years ago our manufacturer for DB was maxed out on capacity. We had to find a backup in order to help us fulfill our orders, so we found one relatively close to our old manufacturer and began a symbiotic relationship with both. From the beginning they assured us that they were excited to work with us and that we were in really good hands. This company was also going through a transition of ownership. After struggling with their branded items, their company was in financial jeopardy and therefore had pivoted into manufacturing for other companies—DB being an example. They had the right equipment and technology, so we placed our trust into a partnership. Not too long after partnering, I was sent a confidential email from someone I trust in the industry with a sales presentation written by our new manufacturer. It included not only a chocolate flavor, but a Vanilla Bean flavor... which was a flavor we had just developed with them! We brought it up to them right away, and they assured us that this had already been in the pipeline and that the recipe was indeed very different to ours. We employed a great legal team to draft up a contract which would prohibit them from using any more of our names/flavors on their products. We proceeded to develop our Key Lime product with them for a special launch with a Florida retailer. At a trade show about six months later, they were showcasing another sweet flavor... something they were calling Lemon Meringue but looked and tasted nearly identical to our Key Lime! But they hadn't breached a contract, having used a different name. We still felt weary but continued to feel out the relationship and hoped for the best. There were several things that unfolded like this, but the final call was when just two weeks after our Pumpkin Pie flavor hit the market, we got wind of another Pumpkin Pie look-alike... to our surprise, it was our manufacturer who had made it! They breached the contract and now gave me no choice but to terminate the agreement. The bummer is that I had already given them access to all of my recipes and intellectual property. Now I knew that their intention all along was to learn and gain information on my clock. While the contract forbids them to use any confidential information that belongs to us, it doesn't mean they can't change one ingredient and call it their own. That's just one challenge of the food industry!

I felt used. They brought us in, made us show them our recipes and processes, and then worked it into their own pipeline for their own benefit. Why would they do this? Why would they jeopardize their relationship with us and also stomp on the innocent creation of DB and our team's hard work? Why wouldn't there be a foundation of respect and care for us as an innovator in the field and group of genuine people who are trying to do good in the world? The answer: fear. This manufacturer was and is in pure survival mode. They have financial goals to hit and therefore they ruthlessly took what they could without any thought of the impact. The impact on our hearts or our business was simply something they didn't give a shit about. It was their families, their paychecks, their wellbeing on the line.

My belief is that businesses operating from this place will disintegrate because the new way is here, and the human species is evolving out of the survival mentality. Our realm is shifting back to our origins in the remembrance of unity and peace.

As much as this situation did impact DB, the real impact is on themselves. I say this with no ill wishes, because truthfully, I want all my fellow humans to thrive and be delighted by life. But it's the truth, right? Their internal world is completely rooted in fear and survival, meaning they are the ones that have to feel it in their bodies each night. We know what it feels like, and we know it isn't fun. They could be free, experiencing complete bliss and collaboration, as well as abundance, if they knew about this new way. If they restored the *heart* within their business.

Every light worker comes in with a specific mission. My mission is to restore the heart into big and small business, because when we do that, the world will indeed change.

My world, for example, has indeed changed! Maria, Jennifer and I have had many opportunities to make decisions from fear. But we overcome our fears by choosing from love, and it works out *every single time.* Our business is thriving and it's fun! It feels like a family. Not only do my team members know how much we care, but my other partners in business know. This isn't about only protecting my company and my family; this is about paving a way for all humans on Earth. It's a big vision, but through the modality of business I know we can do it.

Let's come full circle back to accounting and bookkeeping. I have shared what it looks like to act from fear, so now I will let Maria's and Jennifer's wisdom flow through here so that you can begin to operate from love, specifically when it comes to the finances within your business.

Maria is the founder of her own accounting firm, and she brings a very high vibration and abundant mindset to the books and accounting practices for all of the entities she serves. Maria guards DB's sacred bank accounts and circulation of resources with her wisdom, integrity, connection to God, and her huge heart. Jennifer, DB's other bookkeeping genius works alongside Maria and brings true delight, presence and intuition to our books on a daily basis. Not to mention, both her and Jennifer are total badasses when it comes to the numbers. But for both of them, the way they operate is completely new in the world of finance—meaning they get challenged often and yet continue to pioneer. My hope is that you can utilize the example of Maria and

Jennifer when consciously picking your own CFO, bookkeepers, and "financial guardians."

The frequency, language and intention held when working in our books 100% affects DB's experience of money and sales. Delighted By is first-hand proof that when you invest in a high-vibe accounting team, your sales numbers *will* benefit. It's just like how the vibration of our food affects the health of our bodies, *the vibration and language around the bookkeeping* affects the health of our entities' finances.

I interviewed Maria so that you can pick up some of her golden wisdom.

What do you and your accounting firm "do"?

Maria: *We are very simply an invitation to financial clarity. By bringing high frequency leadership and ground level accounting tools to our clients' accounting departments, we open a space for entities and their founders to thrive and expand.*

To you, what is "the new way" of accounting?

Maria: *Debits and credits will never change. What I believe is changing is that conscious accounting departments will bring way more intuition into the financial analysis, the finance meetings, and the financial decisions. That's not to say that is not already happening at a certain level for many entrepreneurs and their accounting teams, but in the new way it will be more intentional and much more respected. Also, "new way accountants" bring awareness to their beliefs about money, abundance, worthiness and prosperity. When transacting or communicating financial details, they are conscious of their thoughts and feelings and pause if they are contracted or feeling any judgment or fear. They believe in the entities that they serve and listen to those entities for guidance. They bring clarity and accountability to the Founder and hold space for great expansion. The new way accountant, above all, invites everyone away from fear before any financial decision is made.*

Can you speak to the old paradigm of accounting and finance versus the new paradigm?

Maria: *In the old paradigm, many entrepreneurs don't really want to hire bookkeeping help because it doesn't "make them money." They eventually understand that the stress of not being prepared at tax time or the stress of managing tight cash flow takes them away from sales and away from growing their business. They bite the bullet and hire someone to help with the books. They simply hire someone to invoice, pay bills and do payroll. They have no idea how that person feels about money and prosperity or if that person even believes in their entity. In the old paradigm, this bookkeeping help is considered a "cost of doing business." In the new paradigm, the fees of an accounting department are considered an* **investment.** *Entrepreneurs consciously invest in a high-frequency accounting department where the people handling their money are bringing an energy of excellence, service and abundance to all things financial. Their healthy and balanced feelings around money and prosperity will often bring* **more money** *into the business. The accounting department will actually help grow the business—quietly in the background.*

What are the attributes of accounting and finance at Delighted By, specifically?

Maria: *I believe that one of the reasons DB was created was to teach the new way of doing business. And in that purpose, she is constantly challenging those who serve her to do business differently. Regarding accounting specifically—Delighted By is simply asking her accounting team to stay present to the earthly financial needs of a growing business, to be willing to listen to her as she expands and to stay connected to God in all that we do. I try to remember as I review financials and projections that DB is not really interested in what the financials say today because those numbers are all in the past. She is not really interested in our future projections because she always has so much more going on than what we can envision. But she is patient with us. She knows we need to do the projections and that we need to have a plan. We just need to remember to hold on to all of our plans very loosely.*

* * *

A lot of people look at my connection with Maria and Jennifer and wish to find someone similar for their business. To attract in the perfect finance team for you, put your call out to the Universe and follow whatever actions you're guided to in order to connect with the right people. Ask really good questions. This is a completely new way of approaching finance, so maybe you find someone who has never learned the new way but is very open and eager to learn! Don't limit yourself and always use your intuition.

The last thing I'll share here is my personal experience of Delighted By's accounting practices, in the form of a Declaration:

- We do not talk about money from a place of fear. We may acknowledge our fear and release it, but we do so consciously with the intention of shifting it into love before any decision is made.
- We believe in miracles.
- We agree on our core values.
- We lead with an abundant mindset.
- We are guided by Spirit.
- We use intentional, high-vibe language around the money.
- If fear comes up, we go away and realign with the Truth.
- We embody trust.
- We know the truth of where this is going—so this is from where we make our decisions. This is what allows us to keep going, to hire faster, and to make aligned decisions even when the old school biz-people would see it as "too risky."
- As the entrepreneur/chief channeler, I am given freedom

from my finance team to truly and completely *be* in my channel.

- We always work towards unconditional respect for all team members and we openly discuss areas for improvement and admit our mistakes.
- Our purpose for being in business is not to solely be profitable. My team aligns on our mission and the real reason behind our work.
- We do not cut corners to save a buck. We make decisions that align with our values even if it means it costs more or takes more time. Excellence is the name of the game, and we would rather be known for caring rather than be richer because we cut corners.

Another important thing for you to know about the way Delighted By conducts its finances: we always pay our taxes. We don't hire schmoozy tax accountants that can scam the system, instead we hire excellent tax accountants that do it legally and accurately.

Many light workers are extremely opposed to "the systems." The banking systems, the government and tax systems, the education systems. Honestly, I'm right there with you because these systems were all created from fear. However, that doesn't mean you don't have to play within certain parameters when it comes to operating your business. Truthfully, it feels a lot lighter in my body to just pay the darn tax bill, file it accurately, and not have to worry about being audited. Delighted By is the perfect example of merging the two worlds together to create harmony and balance for all.

If you are behind on your taxes, clean it up. The situation may carry a lot of shame, guilt and fear at first, but do yourself the favor of taking this weight off your chest. Remember: tax accountants have seen *everything*. If you are behind, you are definitely not the first person. The last thing you want is to have any guilt, shame or worry attached to your financial situation, whether it's an unpaid bill or failure to file for taxes.

Speaking of systems, remember that every time you make a decision from love, you are influencing the frequency of the money that is flowing in and out of your business. You may despise the powerful four families that rule over all the banking systems of our world, but the reality is that the only thing that can heal this planet is love. If you have a business and you need to have money in a bank, openly and willingly allow the loving frequency of those numbers on the screen to upgrade the system itself. We are not going to heal the banking systems by separating ourselves. Instead, we are going to heal it by bringing love and light to it, unconditionally. I am an idealist, mind you, but I absolutely believe that with patience, deliberation and collaboration, love and unity *will* win. I see Delighted By gracefully upgrading her sweet corner of the system. I, her channel, bring her expression to the world in upmost integrity to her mission. In return, there is an energy exchange — some call it money, but whatever you call it, it is an energetic match to the love DB operates in. This is what I mean. The energy that then hits the bank account is a pure, loving transmission that is doing wonders on the system. Choose from love, not fear, and not only will you and your business be provided for beyond your wildest dreams, but you will be partnering in one of the most important tasks given to our generation: to return humanity's relationship to resources to one that is reverent, pure and sacred.

I have spoken often in this book thus far about how many times I have been initiated into the art of surrender. When it comes to fear around the finances, don't be surprised if your entity brings you up to your edge here. It may help you if you know that you're being tested for a reason that is in your highest interest. If you find yourself up against your primal fear, unsure of how the finances are going to play out, remember the core message of this book — breathe, call on your higher self, and let your heart lead the way. Your nervous system and physical body is actually purging lifetimes of operating from primal fear, so believe me when I say it is very worth going all the way through it. Let yourself feel it all, cry it out, and then when you're ready, stand tall to claim the new path of making decisions from your heart and for the All. As you practice this, it will become second nature.

Chapter 11

When People Screw You Over Plus Legal Talk

I used to believe everyone had great intentions. I had done so much healing work on my heart that I actually started projecting my own behavioral integrity onto others. A mentor and friend of mine, named Stella, told me that there are two types of projection. Negative projection, meaning you take your own fear, insecurity, or discomfort and project it out on to someone else in judgment rather than owning your own experience vulnerably and honestly. And positive projection, meaning you take the positive ways that you operate and subconsciously assume that everyone else around you is going to operate the same way.

In my instance, I assumed subconsciously that everyone is honest, upfront, and well-intended. This is what my inner-innocence wanted to believe, because truthfully the world is a hell of a lot more fun when everyone is operating from their hearts! I would fall in love with people deeply and quickly, sense their good nature, see their gifts, and desire to celebrate them innocently. I took on their advice, their desires, and I'd even adapt to their needs. I would people-please.

My mentor and soul-father, Spiro, warned me at the end of 2016 that not everyone is well intended. He warned me against being so immediately open, especially to those that play into my spiritual curiosity, because oftentimes they are honestly just... using me. Ugh! I was shocked at this advice and didn't believe him at all. My inner child did not want to believe such a thing! In my work with Ayahuasca, she had taught me that love wins. That all people and beings at their core are pure love. I took this lesson very seriously, as I still do, but to my detriment I set aside a key and important gift of being an intuitive human called *discernment.*

A few months after Spiro gave me a bit of a warning, his prediction came true and I was royally screwed over by someone I considered a family member, a mentor, and a business partner in KAKAO. When I began picking up on red flags and bringing these red flags to the table as honestly as a 28-year-old is capable of, this individual revealed her true colors. Spiro was right all along. She had been using me, and her motives were not as pure as she had made out. I was downright devastated about it.

Just like the stories I shared in the previous chapter, this situation didn't come without my own faults and important lessons. But one of my biggest lessons was around the fact that I had been giving my power away. I put this person on a pedestal, doubted my intuitive cues, and people-pleased at the sacrifice of myself and others. And actually, my soul aligned it up this way so that I could begin to heal my mother wound—my fear of letting powerful women down. As soon as the devastating realization played out, I had no choice but to take a stand for not only myself but for my beautiful creation, KAKAO. Once I took this stand and set out clear parameters and boundaries, this person left—for good. I came right up against my core wound of betrayal, which sent me into a healing journey with my inner child that was so needed. I now see the karmic relationship that was playing out and how much it served me, so I am grateful. But that doesn't mean I didn't walk onward with a commitment to using more discernment and to value protective contracts for my entities.

You see, I used to think that legal contracts were silly. I thought they were a waste of money—that lawyers were full of BS, and that all contracts were rooted in fear. I had good intention for avoiding them of course, being that I wanted to exude trust and faith in everyone I chose to partner with and to operate on a foundation of trust and love rather than fears and "what ifs."

In my many experiences over the last five years, including experiences of a manufacturer stealing my recipes, I have discovered a perfect balance regarding legal contracts that works for my heart and at the same time protects what deserves protecting. *Deserves protecting*—that's another thing I took a long time to get. After having a few business deals go wrong due to the fear of others and my lack of clear boundaries, I finally understood and accepted my worthiness in that I am sacred, my businesses are sacred, and we absolutely deserve legal protection. Just like we are currently living in a world that requires businesses to use the traditional banking systems (some exceptions of course), we are also in a time where legal protection is still necessary at times.

My heart's innocence had a really hard time believing that anyone could act from anything other than fairness, kindness, and in thought of the pure mission at hand. To believe that legal protection was necessary would mean that the human collective has not yet reached the point of operating 100% from the heart, which for me was (and is) the toughest lesson I have learned to date. The hardest ceremonies of my life still to this day are around the acceptance of darkness, of evil, and of less-than-pure intentions. My heart yearns for the oneness and unity of our ancient selves. But this specific yearning, and these specific wounds, were mine to heal all along. Thankfully with the support of many mentors, guides, family members and medicine journeys, I stepped into a place of acceptance and therefore freedom from my heart-brokenness.

For most people that have gone through betrayal the way I have, they would probably shift to see the world with a foundation of, *Do not trust anybody.* But that didn't feel right to me. To not trust anybody is pretty standard in the business world, and while I learned that it does have weight, I wanted to find a softer approach that fits my optimistic spirit and feminine heart. I do not ever want to tell an entrepreneur to not trust anybody! Because that tells them to keep their heart closed off to the possibilities of collaboration, family-like bonds, and long-term loyalty. I want to stay in my child-like wonder and openness, while at the same time maintain a healthy dose of discernment and wisdom. Because remember, for every business deal I have had go wrong, I have had at least ten go really, really right.

Here is what I do when any potential business partnership is at hand (i.e. stakeholder, manufacturing partner, or employee):

1. Evaluate the partnership from my heart space. I now take more time than I used to in order to really feel into something. I ask my heart and my business if this is the right person/company. This includes me spending ample time with the person if possible, or at the very least video calls.
2. I draft a list of agreements that are really important to me. I try to think of anything and everything that applies to my mission, to our operating values, to the "what ifs" and beyond.
3. I present this to the potential partner and ask them to give me feedback— are these all things they are able to agree to? If not, why? Do they have something else they'd

like to insert? We work on this together and if all goes well, we finalize a list of agreements that work for both parties.

4. Once we come to an agreement that feels 100% right to me, I take it to the lawyers to work into a formal contract. If we didn't end up coming to that agreement, I move on from the conversations.

5. Upon both parties signing the contract, we begin our partnership with delight and excitement!

One of my friends Joy told me that having someone sign a contract in the very beginning of a partnership will actually take out the chance for them to take it personally. But on the other hand, if you get into a relationship, start noticing red flags, and *then* ask them to sign a contract, it most likely will be taken personally and will bring the distrust to the forefront for both involved. She advised me to do it from the start, and after all of my lessons the last couple of years, I have learned she is most definitely right. Her advice now gets applied to everyone, even if I have known the person for years. If it's a big business deal, there will be a contract, no ifs, ands or buts about it for me these days.

Does my process keep me completely bullet proof? It does not. And the reason is called: soul contracts. Our souls have said yes to working stuff out with other individuals and business entities that will serve the greater good of all. In the instance for myself, the two biggest betrayals were 100% agreed upon by my soul to face my core wound that kept me from being powerful, from shining fully, and from lifting my wings all the way up. In this respect, both of these humans served me more than maybe anyone else ever has—despite the heartbreak and trauma both situations evoked.

No matter what we do to protect our businesses and ourselves, we must always remember that our entity and our soul has a divine plan of service. Sometimes that is to serve us, to serve our employees, or to selflessly serve a company that is needing a serious upgrade in the fear/love department. We must trust this divine plan, while doing everything we can to make sacred agreements at the forefront of partnership.

Sacred agreements at the beginning of a relationship really do set a tone of trust, in fact they allow for *more* trust and connection to play out because both parties have expressed their needs, requests, fears, desires, and a mutual understanding has been developed. If something happens down the road that goes outside the parameters of the contract, it can be addressed cleanly and openly. And sometimes, there is reason to terminate contracts when a breach happens that is outside of your standards. Your entities are sacred, and so is your precious energy. You deserve to be respected, taken seriously and spoken honestly to. If someone steps over your boundaries, there is absolutely nothing wrong with lovingly moving on. You can do this without judgment! You can do it with grace and elegance, in fact. I often tell entrepreneurs that when you say no to what is not in alignment for you, what *is* in alignment for you will fall into place effortlessly.

There have been many times where I have wished for a "conscious lawyer" that would be similar to the way I have partnered with conscious accountants. I believe this sector of work is still very much upgrading out of fear, and that the new way of legal work has yet to be paved, or rather discovered. Let's hold space for that! In the meantime, the legal team I currently work with is a set of women that are for the most part really sweet and understanding of my nature, my dreams and my idealism. They are there to protect me and to tell me what I don't what to hear. No matter what set of lawyers you work with, use your intuition often and let yourself bend the rules if that is what you're genuinely being guided to do. There have been many times in my businesses where I have called in additional mentors to assist with the energetics of business partnerships. And when I say mentors, I don't only mean people that have had successful businesses. The mentors I also like to work with are intuitives and psychics embodied in love, as well as other types of healers. It's nice to gain insight into the entire situation at hand, especially on an energetic level, plus my mentors see into my own soul's contracts and encourage me to grow in certain areas. They often reflect where a certain relationship is mirroring something to me, and where my soul is calling on me to let go of a pattern or embrace a new version of myself. I have become wise enough now to not rely on these types of channels for all of my guidance, but I call on them when I am really stuck. Shout out to all of my mentors—these humans have graciously contributed to my businesses through their personal wisdom and hearts, and also with their divine channels.

Beyond partnerships, another area that the legal conversation may show up in your business is that of trademarks, copywriting, and protecting your intellectual property. If your entity guides you to invest into any of those things, great. Always listen. For DB, we have done it where guided, and I honestly never make it the focus because of my core value of acting from unity, rather than competition and separation. It's important to watch your energy around these types of things, always asking yourself what your true intention is. In my case, when we sign on with a manufacturer now, we do ask them to sign something that shows they won't copy our recipes and/or present similar items to our accounts. This is an integrity thing, truthfully. If a manufacturer charges us to make our product, they should be partnered with us rather than trying to compete with us. Having them sign something like this immediately brings out their true motives, which we have learned to do after experiencing a manufacturer stealing everything out of greed. I feel that recipes and manufacturing partnerships are unique. What I won't do, is get mad or competitive if another food entrepreneur genuinely creates something from their heart and brings it to the shelf, even if it's similar to ours. I encourage and love creativity, diversity and I believe that there is more than enough to go around. This reminds me of when the founder of Allbirds (my favorite sustainable shoe brand) posted on Instagram that he encourages anyone to copy them. He welcomes competition from any shoe company, because he wants to see less plastic in our landfills, and he knows that shoes made from sustainable materials are a revolutionary invention for our Earth. What he does is simply focus on creating badass, unique, sustainable shoes, hiring awesome creative people, and putting out inspiring and engaging content to the world. He doesn't focus on getting everyone to buy only Allbirds, he instead focuses on the greater mission at hand. This is beautiful, and this is what we should all think about if and when we feel we need to protect our creations, our writing, our inventions.

Chapter 12

Using Fear as Your Guidepost and Doing What Scares the Shit Out of You

I f I was asked to give only one piece of advice to an emerging entrepreneur, I would tell them this: *Do what scares the shit out of you.* The fastest way to growth, and to your ultimate success, is by taking yourself out of your comfort zone and into the scary-as-hell terrain called your *dreams*. You know, that dream that you've had in your head for years? The one that people catch you daydreaming of? The one that feels really big, and the one that belongs to you and only you?

It's not so scary just sitting in your head, but when you think of your plan, or the first step to bring it to life, you may think of a million reasons why it's not time yet. Or that it's not possible. That you're not ready. That the world isn't ready.

But the time is now, dear one. I speak to you here assuring you that none of my dreams came true by letting them stay in my head. They came true through inspired action, which I can assure you *really scared me* along the way. I remember one time I was on the way to meet a new potential manufacturer, and I was so scared that I almost didn't get on the plane. My heart was racing, my breath was short... some would call this moment one of intense anxiety. What downloaded into me during this moment of fear was not only the reason why I was able to get on that plane, but also the very reason why I can even write this chapter now. The wisdom I received then is now something I speak to many entrepreneurs about, and it's what I carry with me tightly every time I come up against my own glass ceiling of comfort. Every single thing that I am proud of came from me following my fear. Sometimes the fear is greater than at other times, but the discomfort I view now as a powerful guidepost. It keeps me out of my head and in my heart.

Another word for fear is *resistance,* or you could also call it *self-doubt.* I had resistance in writing and publishing this book, and it took contemplation and growth around my fear of being seen in order to finally bring it to the world. I had fear when booking my flights to Guatemala for the first time. By following that fear, we now impact hundreds of lives through our plant-medicine, KAKAO. I had doubt when I thought of the idea to rent a van and live out of it for a few months to launch DB to the market. Oh my, I can still feel the fear in my bones from when I drove away for the first time! By now you would know that this moment in time for me was an integral part of my journey with DB. Fear, resistance and doubt is present often for me, and I see it as a great thing because it means I am still growing, pushing through my glass ceilings, and pursuing all of my dreams. Now when I feel myself get scared about something, I know that something epic is about to happen! I know that I am being asked to take a leap of faith, to take a jump and to fly to new heights. This is what I mean when I say that you can use fear as your guidepost.

I check myself often on where I am letting fear of the unknown keep me from making a big decision in my business. Recently we had an employee who first of all, I adored for many reasons, and secondly, offered an incredible skillset to DB that at times felt irreplaceable. But time and time again we would feel she was not right for the company. Situations would unfold and I would have the exact same realization—that I think I should let her go. But honestly, I was terrified of doing that out of uncertainty for who would replace her.

When I finally knew that the time had come my body felt like it was such a big, bold decision. Looking back, it really isn't that big a deal in the big scheme of things. But in my body, it felt like a big deal at the time.

The energetic cleansing that my business went through overnight, simply from finally following this guidance and letting this employee go, was palpable by practically the entire team. All of a sudden, there was this free, collaborative, co-creative space we had been yearning for.

Just because a decision you are up against feels scary in your body, does not mean that you aren't meant to make it. And just because it feels like such a big deal today, doesn't mean it will have that level of significance even a week from now. Oftentimes when you take that big leap of faith, you land on the other side with both feet and a sense of relief for choosing to make it in the first place.

I have felt the pitter patter of my heart many, many times when making decisions or choosing to take forward action on pursuing my dreams. In fact, I feel it in my heart right now when I tune into a *really* big vision I have to create my own forward-thinking, technologically advanced, high-vibe food manufacturing facility for the most rad brand and product that has ever presented itself to me. I have talked about DB and KAKAO as my main entities in this book, but I have had a third brewing for a while now. He—yes, he—is an entity I hold very dear to my heart and is the very one that taught me these codes I am about to present to you. His bigness, his complexity, his boldness scares the absolute shit out of me. He has been downloading visions into my heart and mind for the last few years, and the more I "see" the more I wonder *how the hell is that going to happen?*

He answers, "Do what scares the shit out of you. Follow your fear. Take the risk. Be bold. The rest will figure itself out once you claim the dream as yours and pursue it courageously. The money, the people, the support, the clarity, it will all be there, *once you say yes.*"

I am not ready to spill his name, his product, or too much about his vision quite yet, but I do want to pass along his codes to you. The codes that bring me to tears and resonate as Truth in my entire body. The codes that feel dear to my heart, and that I know will continue to bless my big visions, present and future. May they serve you well.

* * *

Deep inside of you is an epic dream.

You were born with this dream—not solely just for you, but for the benefit of all.

Every cell in your being and every atom in the Universe was aligned to support your dream coming true.

Request it and you *will* receive.

I can't promise it'll always be easy.

Bringing your dream to life may have your heart racing 99% of the time.

Chemicals of fear and self-doubt may dump into your system often.

But those are lies.

Remind yourself of this Truth.

Go for it. Breathe deep. Jam out to your favorite music. And get the heck out of your own way so that you can fly.

Request and you will receive.

If your dream scares the shit out of you, say yes to it.

Visualize your dream and then *request it.*

Once you request it, open yourself up to *receive* it!

You can literally do anything you desire to do.

You are co-creating with the Universe to bring the desires of your soul into physical manifestation.

The only thing that can get in the way?

You.

Open your mind, lead from your Truth, surrender to the possibilities, and delight in the entire journey.

Request and you will receive.

You are not alone in pursuing your wildest dreams.

In fact, you are more supported by the Universe and all of its magic than you realize.

The trick to see, feel and hear the support?

REQUEST it!

You will receive guidance.

Find and remember your tools because they'll bring ease and grace into your life experience.

Request for your tools to find you so that you can receive all the assistance you need, that you never even knew was possible.

If you are willing to request, and you are willing to receive, the desires of your soul will be fulfilled.

If you are willing to ask, and you are willing to allow, then you the have the key to living your dream as a reality.

Request and You Will Receive.

This is a story of possibility. **Logic**

Chapter 13

Hiring & Managing a [Loyal] Team

I f someone asked me what the most fulfilling part of having my businesses is, I would answer: my team. Now, if someone asked me what the most challenging part of having a business is, my answer would also be: my team. Not the people in my team per se, but just the inner workings of team dynamics, especially for myself as leading a team was somewhat new for me. I definitely went through growing pains and I continue to learn so much in this area.

Despite the challenges, like I mentioned in the first sentence of this chapter, collaborating with a team is truly rewarding. It's like that for any relationship, truthfully. Many people say that marriage is hard, raising children is hard, being in business partnership is hard, etc. I like to put a positive spin on it and argue that relationships are the key to our personal growth, especially when it comes to our hearts. If you've been heartbroken, you most likely carry those wounds into your next relationship, until you address those wounds fully through love and acceptance and move forward with as open a heart as possible. We have all been there and know how challenging this can be. Some would say that this type of intimate heart-work is meant for your spouse, family, maybe your close friends, but "definitely not in the workplace!" In my businesses, this is *not* the case. Our workplace is indeed a space for us to heal, connect and deepen into our hearts more every single day. Delighted By has called in a diverse group of souls that are playing out soul contracts for their higher self's betterment. Every single one of us has a soul contract with Delighted By, as well as a soul contract with each other. Each one of those dynamics is meant to bring out a different part of ourselves. The ultimate goal for each relationship within the business is absolute harmony. And by harmony I don't mean nodding along or pretending like we all agree with each other. Harmony requires speaking our truth, acknowledging our emotions, being vulnerable, being willing to see things from different perspectives, commitment to growth, and above all, a curious and open heart.

To be in complete harmony amongst the entire team is an ongoing dance. We have never been perfect in all of the ways I outlined above, but it's an important guidepost for us. We are constantly dancing with each other and finding which moves flow in stride, and which ones are lacking grace. Before I get ahead of myself and talk about ways in which to make this dance the most graceful and rewarding, let's talk about the first step in all of this: hiring someone.

Hiring a team is essential to staying in your own zone of genius as the Channel of the entity itself. Delighted By told me early on that I am the Chief Breath-Taker, which also means that all other areas of the business i.e. logistics, sales, marketing, finance, and other operational pieces are *not* meant to be my primary role.

Every entity is so vastly different, so I encourage all entrepreneurs to consistently check in with their own guidance. Every situation is unique because some founders are guided to stay hands-on in many parts of the business for a decade or more, whereas I was guided out of the nitty-gritty sooner so that my energy could be reserved for innovating with new products, creating team culture initiatives, and nurturing the team through one-on-one leadership support. I still get my hands dirty in the various parts of the business, but only when I am genuinely guided to from a place of inspiration (versus fear or worry). This dance is joyful for me now, and I completely trust myself in knowing where I am meant to be involved or when I am meant to get the hell out. The underlying theme of this all is that I have given myself full permission to invest in a badass team so that I can stay in my zone of genius most days.

All entities had their specific team members in mind before conception. As the entrepreneur, the relationship to finding and hiring a team is very similar to the energy of raising capital—it's one we simply must *allow* from a place of curiosity and readiness. Entities call on specific people to not only be served by them, but so that the entity can serve *those specific people in return.* I have witnessed DB and KAKAO radically transform the lives of her past and present employees by doing deep soul work with them. Sometimes this hasn't looked pretty, nor has it necessarily gone the way *I* expected it to go—but one thing is for sure, these entities are fierce in their soul contracts they have with humans on the ground.

Your entity has a soul contract with you, the founder, but also their contracts with other humans. As the entrepreneur/channel, your job is to *respect* these soul contracts and to do everything you can to surrender to them by asking your entity good questions, talking to your own Soul, and looking for the beauty of every situation.

The entities' contracts with other humans have one prerogative: unconditional love. I have watched DB and KAKAO, in their fierceness, invite dozens of humans into shedding layers that keep them from this kind of love for themselves and others.

I have witnessed these entities act like straight-up shamans by bringing up anything and everything that isn't pure light. I have witnessed these entities boot people out when the time was right, completely beyond my own control.

Not all of your employees will know exactly what "conscious enterprise" is at first and that is okay. I as the founder know that DB and KAKAO *channel genius through all of their employees*, but that doesn't mean their employees need to necessarily know that. I have learned that my entities' employees *are not mine.* Entities can attract diverse groups of people with all kinds of language, backgrounds, skillsets etc. I have learned that I must stay completely open to all of the possibilities. As much as I wish that my entities would pick employees who always give a shit about the mission, the planet, and humanity the way I do, that's not always the case right in the beginning. At any rate, it's been a beautiful place to practice unconditional compassion. Because let's face it, humans will be humans. I, along with all of the employees, are learning and shifting each day. As a leader, I have become more accepting and willing to let my employees grow—rather than expect them to be perfect right away. For me, it's when the employees are *not* open to growth that we have to make the tough call to let them go.

This doesn't mean I don't give feedback! I do. I have regular reviews and we openly discuss areas of improvement and requests I may have of them (and them of me!). As the Mother Bear of the team, I trust my instinct and my decisions. While I allow my employees to offer feedback all day every day, I now also know which things I stand firm in and which things are flexible. I always allow this to evolve yet I try not to be wishy washy or unclear in how I communicate what is important to me at the time. I have also learned to try not to prove myself to team members or justify my decisions. The clearer I am in my communication, the better. This means that when I am genuinely unclear about something, I say, "I am unclear right now." To say what I mean and mean what I say is important—for myself and for the entire team. When I am clear, I share my clarity and own it as my truth without the need for validation or approval. This is an empowerment thing that I have learned over time and am still embracing further with each day. Some people call this compassionate leadership or collaborative leadership.

I lead my conversations with employees from my heart. I want to know how they are, how they're feeling, what they've been experiencing in all areas of their lives, and any feedback they have for both me and/or the organization. Delighted By, being such a pure expression of unconditional love, has told me on many accounts that she loves doing heart-work on people. So, when you get triggered by people within your organization that don't lead with their heart the entire time, be assured that the entity is working on them in this way. And of course, not all contracts are permanent. Hiring, managing and firing is 100% guided and oftentimes not how we would expect it to go. Personally, this has been one of the toughest parts of the business, because it's an area where I often have to completely *let go of control* and simply trust.

A keynote here on team communication, which I have learned through being a part of a virtual team (no physical office) the last five years. My belief now is that emails and texts are for information exchange, not true communication. And it's case to case basis. I have some employees and partners in business who are incredibly receptive to email communication of all kinds, whereas for others it just creates way too much resistance and a clashing of energies. Especially for big decisions and vulnerable expressions, use in-person, the phone or video conferencing. It is the harder thing to do sometimes (scarier) but it's also the right thing and creates way more ease long-term. I now deliver direct feedback through phone conversation or in person only, so that I can hear the way they take it and support them through their process. You can live by the rule that all feedback, large decisions, and complex communications cannot be done via email. I have learned this the hard way, so I want to save you from my mistakes.

Delivering big stuff through email is a fast way to make your team hate you, quite honestly. I have found myself apologizing many times for putting something in email versus over the phone, which I realized I was doing mainly because we are a virtual company on many different time zones. It now helps to remember that nothing is truly urgent, and that if I have an important thing to say or converse about, I can wait until we find a mutual time to talk as a team or one-on-one. This is the same for anyone you are working with in business, whether it's vendors, suppliers, customers etc. Just know that something in writing can get misinterpreted in many different ways, so it's better to use voice and dialogue. I now also refrain from discussing ideas or potential solutions via email, because it creates long threads of complexity and everyone that is cc'd often gets confused (including myself). Call a meeting and open the conversation. Way simpler and in the end produces a quicker, more efficient result.

When going into the hiring process (or wanting to go into the hiring process!), think really, really big. Let yourself dream of all the support you desire. You deserve it, and if you're dreaming about it it's because it is part of the vision! Give yourself more permission to hire and delegate. Do not let money fears make any decisions when it comes to hiring. Tune in deeply to your intuition for all decisions regarding hiring and salaries. Loosen your grip to let your entity fly even more. Only do work within your business that you are genuinely delighted by. Hire and delegate out all the areas of your business that you know you are *not* delighted by. Write letters to those you are desiring to call in for team members, similar to what we discussed for calling in aligned investors. Alternatively, list out all the attributes you are looking for in someone including their skillsets, and at the bottom write in big letters, *this or better.* Be open to meeting your entity's employees in unique, non-traditional ways.

In interviews, express your personal intention with your entity and the values you desire to be upheld within your organization. Ask really good, unique, guided questions. Remember that your entity *is* sacred, so be wary of rushing into anything—unless you're guided to of course! Be fully expressed in all periods of interviewing, hiring, managing, and firing. Transparency, heart-centered communication, and honoring your own emotional processes/intuition is the key to complete freedom in your leadership.

Remember you are not the boss, *your entity is.* So, if things get tough with team-members, go to your boss. They always provide sound and clarifying energy for you to share, reveal, ask and receive wisdom through. It's like a quarterly review with your boss: you and your entity, where you express any and all concerns and feelings; where they gently but fiercely give you feedback; where you leave feeling like there is nothing in between you and them or you and the employees; where you go forward with a new perspective and new awarenesses to integrate into your leadership. When you are clear emotionally, you will be guided with ease and grace, even when the decision is a tough one or one that requires tremendous Surrender.

Last but not least: Give it back to Mother Earth. She is here to catch all of your human-as-fuck feelings, mess-ups and emotions. This has been a *key piece* of my journey when dealing with other humans—aka managing a team. When we give it back to her, she replaces our nervous systems with compassion, grace, forgiveness, unconditional love, wisdom, strength, courage and Truth. She is here to catch us, so that we don't have to hold it all. We were never meant to do this all alone, which brings me to the next section of this chapter.

Embracing Your Spirit Squad

While our entities have human team-members, we also have access to other help and assistance: that of our "spirit squad." Our spirit squad is our invisible team of helpers that desire to be known, acknowledged, and called on so that they can fulfill their purpose: to serve us and make this a whole lot easier down here. Our spirit squad certainly includes our entity itself, yet beyond our entity, we also have a heap of angels, guides, animals, plants, earth-energies, and multidimensional energies that can be called on in any and every situation.

When shit hits the fan, I notice that the human tendency is to get in our heads about it and "try to figure it all out." I am certainly guilty of this. I have first-hand experience of just *how much easier* it can be when I simply call on my spirit-squad. Here are some examples:

I ask Gaia, the spirit of Mother Earth in dragon form, to come to all sales meetings with me. Before I even get there, I ask her to calm the nervous systems of the people I'm meeting with, so that by the time I get there they are more likely to be in their heart as opposed to their mind. It goes without saying that I have never had a buyer tell me "no" in a sales meeting.

I asked Archangel Michael to walk onto the Shark Tank set with me. I asked for his protection and light to surround my entire body. He ended up being the one who told me to say yes to Mark Cuban in the midst of the heated conversation, as my human self was completely at a loss of what to do.

I call on all my angels and guides to be on the trucks carrying my products while they're in transport, so that the vibration of the hummus is protected every step of the way. I ask them to block out any dark or dense energies that could come from any of the drivers, truck stops, or surrounding products.

I have "marketing angels" at every store the hummus is at, bringing beams of light to the product so that those who are ready to receive it, see it and gravitate to it.

I ask my angels and guides to be with my employees 24/7.

I call on angels of light to be at every production run of hummus, and I see them sprinkle glitter and light through all of the machines, ingredients and tubs. Spreading my glitter at its finest.

I have called on my angels and guides in times of panic, so that they could sort out all the details without me needing to lose sleep or stress my nervous system out. We avoided a nationwide recall this way, when I had fairies go into every batch of hummus and re-upgrade it with the glitter and light it had been birthed in.

I have finance angels too, that wrap up our bank accounts in protective light in order to avoid leaks or holes in those accounts.

I ask my angels and guides to sort out shipping issues, packaging mistakes, and even emails that come through at 10:00 p.m. that I just know wouldn't be in alignment for me to answer at that time. *Every single time*, without fail, I wake up to everything being completely sorted.

DB is certainly part of my spirit-squad—she is the chief angel. I call on her wisdom and assistance constantly. Do things go differently than I had planned or expected? Absolutely—but in the long term it is *always for the better.* All of the angels have it. They have this whole thing on wraps—but we have to *ask them.* Ninety-nine percent of the time I "go general" and just ask them to "have it all," which is totally acceptable, and it works too. But *being specific is of huge benefit.* My incredible mentor, Spiro, once told me that our spirit guides desire us to be really specific. It's how they can help us the most, which is all they really want to do.

The best way to play with this is just simply try it out. Maybe you can't see, feel or hear your spirit guides yet, but it won't hurt to simply try asking them a question or requesting their support on something that matters to you. It's similar to talking to and hearing your entity's voice in that the more you do it, the easier it gets and the more apparent that something magical really is occurring behind the scenes.

Nurturing Your Diving Feminine Is the Greatest Investment in Your Business

I get more "done" in my business when I start each day with ceremony and practices that honor my physical, emotional, mental and spiritual wellbeing. If I wake up and start on emails right away, only 1/100th gets accomplished versus when I start my day with me-time, phone free, a cup of cacao in hand and a journal and pen to write with. I meditate, put on the essential oil diffuser, sometimes do breath-work, talk to my entities, and overall tune into my body.

To have a daily self-care ritual for yourself is super important, no matter who you are. But as an entrepreneur, having a daily ceremony with and for your entity is a beautiful practice that pays great reward. During daily ceremony with my entities, I bring my attention to everything going on, in, and around the business. The good, the bad and the ugly, I bring it to the table here. I write out my intentions, and I envision. As I sit there, with intended focus on each area (i.e. certain team members, new product launches, production issues, logistics changes, raising capital etc....), not only do I gain new awareness and perspective on each area, but I get to dream with my entity and literally see the future. It may sound crazy, but I swear that when I do this and sit in the dreaming, the visioning itself, all of the details get sorted out with ease, grace and delight. This actually happened today! In the last couple of weeks, I have been dedicating part of my morning meditations to switching DB's packaging over to a much more sustainable, plastic-free option. I have been envisioning the miracle and the transition happen and guess what—when I finally was ready to bring the initiative up to my manufacturer, the CEO affirmed that they were already working on the very solution of clay/ceramic pots we had been looking at!

Honestly, I am still in shock and amazement. My biggest worry for our 2020 sustainability initiative had been that our manufacturer would say it's not possible—I thought we would have to make long, well-prepared presentations about how these initiatives are beneficial for all involved, etc. I had noticed this worry in my body, which is why for a couple of weeks in meditation I had been working to switch that vibration of limitation to the vibration of limitless possibilities. I envisioned the manufacturer being open, willing and ready to make this miraculous transition happen until I finally believed in my cells that it *would* be possible without resistance. Once I brought myself into vibrational alignment with my dream of switching away from plastic tubs, I then verbally expressed the initiative and shared my passion behind it. Now this dream is becoming a reality, completely resistance free. Wow! Pinch me.

This is the magic of our "divine feminine"—whether you're a male or female, we all have access to this creative power. This is why I see all of my down-time, my cacao ceremonies, my walks in nature at 1:00 p.m. and my weekly float-tank sessions as *genuine investments in my business.* Because it's in these sacred moments that my heart is wide open, and my creative force is bursting in such a high vibration. This is the Law of Attraction at its very finest.

Personal alignment happens when you're genuinely happy and nourished in every area of your life. For me this sometimes did look like working for twelve hours straight, because I was lit up by my vision and was just so inspired to create constantly. Over time, it was clear that my body and my soul desired more down-time, connection time, and nature time. At first, I was scared that working less would mean less results, but no—my guides emphasized over and over again that *when I am in my Divine Feminine power, this is when the real shit gets done.* Wow, how cool is that.

In most of my journey with Delighted By, I have taken really,

really good care of myself. Even when my bank account was negative, I still always found a way to receive nourishing energy from Mother Earth, to eat organic food, to attend Aya ceremonies, and to take days off of technology when guided to. There have been many times where I have failed to listen to my body and I kept going despite my higher guidance, due to fear and learned patterns... but I promise you *this never turned out well.* It looked like complete overwhelm, total burnout, and massive tantrums. After this happened enough for about two months straight, I came back to my radical alignment by hiring three extra team members and heading to Australia to nourish my body, nurture my relationship with Michael, and serve KAKAO to our tribe on a tour. To the rest of the world, this could have appeared as irresponsible, but for me, there was nothing in the world that could have felt better. I accepted that I had been called to pioneer conscious enterprise, which includes me being in radical alignment with my Soul. As I write this I am sitting in the Blue Mountains of Australia. I have never felt more aligned, because not only is my body relaxed, my mind creative, and my Soul happy, but also DB is truly thriving back in the USA. Her team of ten is completely in their zone of genius, and gracefully owning their roles. I check in with DB every day, and DB assures me she is flying, she is delighted, and she wants me exactly where my true power lies: in my alignment.

Looking back, I never would have gotten to this severe stage of burnout in the first place if I would have listened to my body earlier. But it was in my journey and through the contrast where I learned, so I am grateful for that destiny and for where I am now — with a much greater sense of work-life balance and peace.

How to Deal with Other People's Opinions in Your Biz

Your entities are *your* entities. When you start a business, you may find that there are people who want to contribute their ideas and/or opinions. I've learned that it's important to set really clear boundaries for myself when it comes to taking on others' opinions, thoughts and ideas, while of course staying open to the wisdom that the Universe may be dropping you through various means.

I was speaking to my friend, Jenny, founder of her nonprofit CelebrateEDU about this several weeks ago. We were agreeing that it throws us off a bit (or at least it used to) when hearing other people's thoughts—even positive ideas—about our businesses. When you are approaching business in a new way and embodying the Conscious Entrepreneur's Creed, it is so important that *you* honor yourself as the channel by tuning into your own deep intuitive knowing and only acting from there. There are of course times where your entities have chosen to channel a message through someone else, to be of your benefit and assist you in the process. Simply bring intention to this space. Check in.

Here's how I check in: If it makes me *go to my head*, I know that it's not my entity. So, for instance, when I sat down with Mark Cuban, he gave me a lot of ideas and ways on how DB could be run—all super positive ideas from a place of contribution on his part (damn, he is *so* smart). But I would walk away from the time with him more confused, more in my head space, and feeling like I need to "figure it out" or force something in order to take on the ideas he presented. This feeling in itself was a message from DB saying, "that's not me telling you that; it's someone else's voice." Any time my mind gets involved from a place of overwhelm or imbalance—versus divine mind and clarity— that's when I know it's not DB.

Humans are birthing business entities now in ways that have never been done before (or if they have been done before, they haven't been talked about, acknowledged or recognized as Truth by larger society standards). So, for instance, when we talk about an endless supply of abundance; when we talk about not leading from fear; when we talk about the new way of raising capital—

these are very new concepts that you and your entities have signed up for to embed into the planet. Remember this when you go out to lead and live out your business. The way that you do it will most likely be questioned by the outside world *and oftentimes by your own mind*—because you have your own belief systems from society and past conditioning.

Right now, as I write this paragraph, I am hiring new leadership for DB. Based on our business history and timeline, it's considered by the biz world to be very "early" to do this. It may be viewed as irresponsible; it may be assumed that I have "lost motivation" or I "can't focus"—classic things the business world says about entrepreneurs. When in reality, I am *hearing to my core* that my entity is calling in new leadership, and that the best way I can serve her is to actually *listen.* She comes through my body, my ceremonies, and my meditations and reminds me to ignore what everyone else is saying, including my own mind, so that I can follow this divine guidance she is giving me.

When you say yes to your entity, you get to tap into what *you* desire your reality to be. If you want your reality to be abundant, easy, playful, free and fun, then your entity will absolutely be on board with that. Just remember that the outside world may have their own opinions about this—calling you irrational. You are being asked to pioneer this new paradigm so that in twenty years from now, give or take, there will be entrepreneurs looking to you and me as examples. Because this new way will be just *the* way. Choosing to do it from a place of guidance, of tapping into the wisdom of Spirit, of acting from a place of abundance, of opening up our channel, and of respecting Mother Earth—all of these values that you and I embody will eventually be looked at as *the way.* But you have to stick to them, and you have to commit to being the pioneer of them.

Now that so many people know about Delighted By, we get a million and one ideas—always well-intentioned, but I have chosen to wrap myself up energetically. I have gotten to know DB so intimately that nothing can rock us and our messages. There is no one, at this stage, not even Mark Cuban, my investors, the press, or my employees, that can rock what I know is true. I have really practiced the communication with DB, and we have this bond. I am now very clear when she is speaking to me. I know when she is trying to speak through someone else, and I know when she isn't.

To recap, know that embodying *ease* in business may get some resistance from others. The tighter you bond with your entity, the more you'll know what is your entity's voice and what isn't. I am learning more every day that I don't have to choose for it to be hard. The clearer you are in your choices, the more you will be met with support and honor by the outside world. It's incredibly powerful to be the pioneer of these concepts because it will no doubt affect future generations. You are genuinely giving energetic permission to live the new way. Your embodiment of this, in itself, is the permission.

Leadership Codes for the Conscious Entrepreneur

Most of the DB Team came together for the first time in the flesh last year, considering we operate as a remote company. It was such a receiving for me because by being in person, every one of the team members got to *feel* and breathe in the actual ethos of this company.

It's one thing to have talked about it on a million zoom meetings, but for them to sit in circle with me brought it to a new place for everyone, including myself. It's like all my "woo-woo" talk that they may sometimes brush off as the "owner's crazy spiritual lingo" actually became *medicine*, because it hit their hearts through KAKAO, deep conversations, real in-person confrontations, adventure, sound healing and yummy feasts.

I used to resist the food industry so much, one reason being that the humans we employ come from more traditional backgrounds, meaning them working for DB requires total surrender and trust of something different... which sounds beautiful right here, but honestly it has been challenging for them at times! You can't convince someone to step into their healing; you can't convince someone that it's going to be worth it; and especially being someone's employer, you cannot convince an employee that this new way of doing business (from love, not fear) actually works. They honestly just have to stick it out and get proof for themselves, over time. Some people make it, some people don't. And the humans on my team now have done just that.

I've been met with resistance over and over again, from myself and my team, yet what always resided at the core of all of us was a commitment and a curiosity (at least enough for them to stick around). When something goes "wrong" in the business and I invite an employee to look deeper into the situation to see where they are creating it themselves... is confronting for them to say the least. Drama between team members, frustration towards manufacturers, fear around not having the standard "systems" in place that offer surface-level security... I could list here a million things that come up in this environment that invite us all inward. You have to imagine the true shock that happens to an employee when they start working for me. Some positive shock like, "could this really be true?" Because it feels so good and free to speak their vulnerabilities, to share their feelings, and to be led by someone that isn't driven by money. And some negative shock like, "wait, I signed up for a job to collect a paycheck, not to be confronted by my closet of bullshit that I've been trying to hide away for twenty years." It is pretty hilarious when reflecting on it in this way. My poor employees! I have put them through hell by asking them to dive into their own fire, so that ultimately, they could rise into who they always were before society and corporate America conditioned them. DB has invested in their growth through coaching, monthly breathwork, and more... and they have invested too. They have chosen to continue coaching, go to personal development courses, to speak up even when they're scared, and to trust me.

The most fulfilling thing for me as a Founder is to witness each of their journeys. I am currently in the process of presenting to investors and it's kind of hilarious, because the thing that I really like to speak to isn't the numbers or the exit strategy, but rather the team's inner growth. I just know we are making a difference in the world by cultivating true heart-centered leaders (myself included) within this container of DB. This is what I care about, and it is the very thing that fills my cup.

These core values below — sticking to them — have contributed to the greatest growth and expansion for the team. I am also listing some other pointers based on what I have learned in this past year in terms of managing a team and leading a business.

1. Encourage everyone to say what they are actually thinking.

2. Provide a safe space so that it can get messy. I encourage my employees to let it get messy between each other, so that nothing goes unheard. As a leader, my job is to cultivate the ceremonial container in which they can do this. I now act as the momma bear because I do my own work with every team member, meaning I see nothing but their Soul and absolute Truth when I see them. So, when drama arises, I can sit from a higher perspective of love and support while everyone works out their stuff. To be clear, I have my own stuff arise with nearly every one of my employees… and what do we do with it? We work on it. My current team members are with DB not just because of their credentials or skillsets, but because they sat in the fire with me and cultivated an even deeper bond. I call this The DB Initiation.

3. Stick to exactly who you are and trust your intuition. For me, this sometimes means *not* rescuing my employees or

hopping on a meeting with them right away. Sometimes it means letting them sit in the fire so that I don't take it on in my own body. And these days it means owning my role of creator/visionary and staying out of the nitty gritty unless DB really asks me to. I choose very selectively which meetings to show up to, that's for sure. This doesn't mean I don't show up for DB and what needs to be acted on. I one-hundred percent have to show up and remember that my voice, my presence and my heart's vision must be imprinted into the team weekly. It's a balance and I have had to cultivate a very deep listening of when to step forward, and when to step back.

4. Trust your team's brilliance and release control of doing it all on your own. Know when *not* to speak or delegate and trust yourself completely when you feel it is a time to direct the ship.

5. Be direct. No sugarcoating of the truth. I always listen to the team members' perspectives and remember their voice as I go forward in leading. Every day I learn something new and let my employees shape me into a better, more compassionate leader. The clearer I am in my directives, the clearer their response. If I am confused or in self-doubt, they will meet me with resistance. If I am owning my power and my leadership with clear, directive communication from my strong, confident knowing, this is typically where I am met.

6. Gain counsel when you are confronted. Whether it's from an outside mentor, from Gaia, or from sitting longer with your Soul. Sitting before acting and speaking has been a huge lesson for me.

7. Don't rely on yourself to coach your employees all the time, instead tune in to know which modality or person may be best for them and offer it. The Landmark courses and working with various mentors has been key for most

of my team. Sometimes DB pays, sometimes she doesn't, because I want to see that the employee is invested in themselves. I hate it when we pay for something and the employee doesn't choose to embody the wisdom they learned, so I now lean on my intuition here, and yes sometimes it is a risk! Many times it is so worth it.

8.   Tune into the entity constantly on who and what is right for DB and honor the soul contracts. Sometimes this means keeping someone on board when the world is telling you to fire them. Other times it means letting them go when your entire heart is breaking at the thought. Every employee is different and there is no rule of thumb here because it's all a soul contract between the entity and the employee. I honor these contracts greatly and I surrender my fears completely to let that contract play out. I get questioned all the time about my team and why I chose certain people to do certain things, and honestly it all comes down to one answer: guidance.

9.   Last but not least, do your very best to encourage calm nervous systems, especially in such a fast-paced world. At DB we do monthly breath-work workshops; I point out to an employee when I feel an email was rushed or from a place of stress; and I lead by example by never drinking coffee and knowing that my breath is the most important thing I could offer to the DB workspace. My team is now so attuned to my nervous system that they can feel when I send something out of fear, and they call me on it whether telepathically or verbally. It's a beautiful accountability system we've got going now.

Letting the Role in Your Business Evolve Plus Receiving the Gift of Your Entity

Delighted By called on me to birth her into the world. I answered her calling with fierceness, and now just five years after her birthday, she is fully functioning on a national scale without me micro-managing or participating in every single meeting.

How did I go from making hummus in my own kitchen eight hours per day and running the other parts of the business for another eight hours per day, to now having the full, diverse experience of being a multi-passionate entrepreneur, delighting in my sacred union with Michael, playing around the world, writing this book, preparing myself to be a mother one day, birthing new creations, taking care of myself, cooking fresh plant-based meals every day, and still nurturing my team, my loved ones and my community?

The answer: I let my role with DB consistently evolve and change, and I granted myself the permission to *receive* her as much as I give to her.

I remember when DB initially started asking me to layer my leadership and bring on more support. But I was scared that if I wasn't hustling hard or struggling in some fashion, she may not provide for me. Or, if she *does* provide for me, I wouldn't have earned it in the way I had before. Who am I to be worthy of that?

I had two Ayahuasca ceremonies in these months and the themes of them were: *How much love can you let in?* and *How much light can you let in?* In these ceremonies, Delighted By and Aya taught me to receive more deeply. I of course had been through dozens of initiations on "receiving" at this point, but this time was different. DB showed me all the work I had done for her and with her. She showed me just how much we had done together. She showed me and had me feel just how much *she loves me.* She thanked me and told me it was all for me to learn to receive.

And boy does it feel like a receiving to me. To receive Delighted By is one of the most intense, invigorating, heart-opening experiences I have ever had. To look back at the journey thus far, to feel into everything I've learned and continue to learn, to realize that Aya has been such a main component of it all, to tap into every beautiful soul I have met through her, and to know what we are pioneering together... *that* is what I receive. I feel incredibly blessed to be financially provided for through DB, yes, but that doesn't scratch the surface of what I'm fully receiving... I am receiving pure, unconditional love from a master, non-physical entity. The biggest thing that I receive is *the fact that she chose me.* Who am I to receive her? To be chosen by her? How could I possibly be this blessed? I couldn't have dreamed of her fullness even if I would have tried. I never could have come up with the magical journey and the depth of her. No "law of attraction" practices could have brought the perfection of DB into life. You seriously can't write this stuff—you cannot make it up.

These entities are here to give to us. And we are chosen by them *to receive them.* One beautiful way we can receive our entities is by letting ourselves be in our full Zones of Genius, coined by the awesome author Gay Hendricks in his book *The Big Leap.* A must-read for any entrepreneur, in my opinion, A regular practice of mine was inspired by the wisdom Hendricks offers in this book. It looks like me asking myself these questions as often as possible:

1. *Am I residing in my Zone of Genius 100% of the time?*
2. *Where am I acting in my Zone of Excellence or Zone of Competence?*
3. *Where am I "upper limiting" myself from experiencing even more joy, creativity, fun, abundance and fulfillment?*
4. *Where am I being a victim of a limiting belief?*
5. *What could I delegate out today that isn't the best use of my creative energy?*
6. *What parts of the business am I no longer enjoying?*
7. *What parts of the business do I want to learn more about or invest more time into?*

My work with my entities and my creations have demanded

that I stop comparing myself to other entrepreneurs and light-leaders. There are so many people out there doing really badass things, but our individual journeys are unique, and they deserve our reverence, versus constant comparison to the journey of others. Rather than living from "the grass is always greener on the other side" mentality, we have the opportunity to receive the epic tapestry that is our side. As you embark on your entrepreneurial career, refrain from comparing your journey or personal experience with anyone else's. We were all designed so uniquely, just like our entities were. In short, as your relationship and roles change throughout your entrepreneurial career, don't ever shame yourself if it doesn't look like the next person. As you allow yourself to fall deeply in love with *the Beloved within*, and with the heart of your entity, you will learn to embrace your unique brushstrokes more and more.

Chapter 14

Creativity: Artfully Turning Your Human Experience into a Lasting Legacy

Every single human on this planet is inherently creative. We are creative beings, simply put. We can create art and music, yes, but we can also create solutions, writings, businesses, products, events, offerings and families.

If you feel stuck creatively, or don't see yourself as a creative person, it's probably just because you haven't embraced or accessed this part of yourself yet.

In the first part of this chapter, I want to explain more about creative energy and how to harness it. This conversation is so important because we are in a time where our creative energy is needed more than ever. From reversing climate change to healing the collective feminine and sexual repression, our solutions through this creative force are being called upon. Plus! It's so fun and fulfilling to be in your full creative expression! It feels juicy, alive, playful and energizing.

If someone would have asked me back in college if I am a creative person, I probably would have said no because I am not an artist by the traditional definition. But now, I feel like one of the most creative people I know. I am tapped into my creative force every single day and when I access it, I come alive. I have many parts to myself, but my creative self is one of my favorite spaces to play in. Creativity can come through daily in cooking, writing, forming a structure for a meeting, envisioning the future, and more.

What is creative energy? Creative energy is your life force and it has the potential of moving up through you and out into the world. Some speak about creative energy as chi, sex energy, prana, or source energy. Yes, you can use your sexual nature as a human to inspire and express creativity! In fact, that is why it's there. To create physical babies, yes, but also to create energetic babies/offspring (businesses, ideas, art, poetry, letters, and more).

I found that the more I healed my lower chakras and womb space, the more creative I became. This goes for anyone—to remove baggage, trauma, and pain from this sacred container of the body will create more room for the pure and potent energy of creation to rise within you. This also means that the more open I am to this energy, or more receptive should I say, the more creative I am. In other words, if you are shut down in your lower chakras or resistant to sex energy/pleasure as sacred and pure, then you may be blocking your creativity as well. Once you open these channels again through healing, purification, and awareness, you can bring this energy up and through your heart space as a beautiful expression for the world to benefit from. Now, what you will create is not always up to you! It's not something you think about or get in your head about, it's something that *falls* on you or *rises* in you and can feel quite spontaneous. It's your job to welcome it, ensure there is fertile soil for it to plant in, and then take inspired action when it presents itself clearly.

There are many meditations and breath-work practices you

can do to open to this energy and allow it to move in service to the Divine. In addition, communing with nature will help this energy arise and stir within you. Mother Earth is a representation of the womb of creation so you can receive what I call "creation codes" from her directly, just as I have!

Most recently, I have received what I now call "Innovation Codes," which carry the principle that one should only innovate from pure inspiration—meaning the innovative idea *falls* on you, rather than you creating it from your mind.

To innovate out of the mere intention to make money, get ahead of the competition or "stay on top," is a less than pure place that I encourage every entrepreneur to be wary of. These Innovation Codes also carry the principle that *depth within inventions* will always be more important than quick, gimmicky inventions.

Here is a real life example. At Delighted By, I created a core lineup of dessert dips that use 100% natural ingredients and that came from genuine inspiration. The industry on the other hand, tells me that in order to stay on top, to be one step ahead of the big guys, I need to keep inventing new flavors that the masses will deem trend-worthy and novel. My current flavors are simple yet awesome: Brownie Batter, Red Velvet Cake Batter, Mint Chocolate Fudge, Vanilla Bean, Snickerdoodle Cookie, Key Lime Pie and Pumpkin Pie. But I had some people tell me that if we *really* want to stay cutting-edge, we need to make more, do more, be more—with flavors that the middle of America will love, such as Cookies & Cream, Yellow Cake Batter, S'Mores, etc. While those sound delicious, the idea of these flavors didn't *fall* on me organically… nor can they be created without using some bullshit "natural flavoring" which is just another way of saying MSG. It took a lot for me to stand in my truth and trust that if DB really wanted these types of flavors to be created, she would tell me, and I would feel super inspired by them. Honestly, I *tried* to get excited by these flavors because intellectually, and financially, it made sense. But in my heart, and in my gut, I heard a no. So instead, we are focusing our energy on creating more *depth* of what we already have by investing our time and resources into a four-Phase Sustainability Initiative that lights my soul up! We are also directing energy on touching more customers with the current flavors we have, because we haven't even begun to touch the full potential of them. I am so excited to go deeper and to leverage the solid foundation we have worked so hard to build, rather than scurrying around and mentally "innovating" to stay on top of the trends and make a quick dollar. That is not how any of my creations came to life, and I am committed to that now and forevermore.

Creativity is for men and woman, and as a collective we are awakening to this truth more than ever. If you desire to be more creative, just say your intention out loud and believe me, it'll happen.

I see creative expression as my way for leaving a lasting legacy of love on this planet. I love to bring my joy and gratitude through a creative expression, and I also have learned to heal my pain and less-than-blissful moments through creative expression. In fact, when I do, I transmute the pain and use it *for good*. To utilize your human experience as a means for creativity is a superpower we all have, and in my opinion, one of the most healing tools we can access for ourselves and for the world.

When I am confronted with something challenging or uncomfortable, I give it my attention so that I can feel it, release it, and let it go. But as a human, I have found that *some things* are so big and memorable that we can't simply let them go forever. How can I forget, be completely done with, the loss of my best friend for instance? The betrayal by my own mother? Am I meant to arrive at some point where the thought of these things doesn't impact me at all? And what about war? Poverty? Rape? Animal Cruelty? The greed and fear that steals from the lands of our Momma Earth? Am I meant to be so evolved that I am not affected by those things?

The romantic, human heart in me is stirred deeply by the longing for unity, and my human emotions in this lifetime that remind me of anything but unity, encourage me to put my love into expression. Maybe if I sing my song of grace for longer, we will stop killing our brothers and sisters in wars over land and money. Maybe if I dance in grace for longer, we will return to nature and in harmony with our planet. Maybe if I spread more of my glitter, my glitter of grace, all men and woman will unite together in forgiveness and respect. Maybe if I create another fun product, vision, team, poem, book or podcast episode with a wide open heart, I will call out to my fellow humans and they will listen. They will awaken. They will eventually hear. They will remember. We will unite. Love will win. This is the truth of how this story will end.

Not only will this story end in love, but it will be our creative expression and our pure, humble, high-frequency service to the All that we'll be able to thank for it. God/Goddess will stir wisdom and light within us. And through our purified vessels and open hearts we will bring these blessings out into the world that needs it the most.

My anxiety, grief, fear, anger, sadness, confusion, hurt and suffering will continuously be transmuted on behalf of the entire collective through my art.

My joy, abundance, connectivity, delight, gratitude, grace, celebration, compassion, forgiveness, play and freedom will continuously bless this planet through my being, through my expressions, through my feeling, through my creating.

My life is my canvas. I make it my own, without any rules or limitations. I flow, I discover, I admire, I smile as I let Spirit paint a magical picture through my earth-walk. In my Being, the masterpiece of my life only becomes more beautiful. The depths of my heart is in every single tub of hummus, every cup of KAKAO, every post on our KAPU app. The pain of my past becomes my empowerment, and my empowerment is passed on through my products, businesses and expressions. The more I experience in life, the more I become myself. And the more I become myself, the more multi-layered and magnificent my external expressions are.

My creativity is a key way I leave a legacy that lives beyond my human form. Which is why I make sure I express it in ways that stick. I find fertile soil to create in, and an environment in which it can thrive. I set aside the temptation for instant gratification and immediate feedback for my creations, and instead choose bolder, stickier, life-lasting expressions. Like this book. Or my companies. Or my future brick-and-mortar chain of cacao cafes. Oh, what disservice I would have done to the world and my future children if I took my moment of inspiration and channeled it into an Instagram post, or worse, let my fear get the best of me and withheld my soul's song altogether.

There is a focus and dedication I carry that comes from the deeper parts of me who realizes that we as a human race have genuinely betrayed ourselves. We have fallen asleep and turned a blind eye to protecting the innocence within. We have completely abandoned what is right and true! We have been fighting the wrong fight! We have gotten so caught up in a rat race and allowed severely wounded leaders to lead us astray. But it wasn't "they" versus "us." It was *we*. We did this to ourselves, and now it is the time to bring us out of it. By harnessing the creative power within each of us is how we do it. There will be no one left behind, which implies that we will need some serious man/woman-power here! We need you, me, and everyone else who has been blessed with the opportunity to heal their personal wounds, to bring their attention to the collective with a focused warrior spirit and a dedicated heart. We must be in our pure alignment and joy, sitting from a higher view so that we don't become the chaos below. From this higher place, you will be positioned to spread massive amounts of glitter. It's beautiful up here. So beautiful that we really should invite the entire world to check it out. Why have we been sinking down and letting ourselves struggle day in and day out?

I led you into the battlefield so that I could teach you how to fight the right fight. And now I am walking you right back out of it because you have learned everything you need to learn. You have been initiated, time and time again. You have gone through death and rebirth, and it is my hope that you fully utilize this mastery in the rest of your alchemization and rebirth processes throughout your life. You have realized that you deserve to be happy, to be free, to think for yourself, to know magic directly, and to be genuinely delighted by life!

You are ready now. To spread your glitter in a way that has never felt so good, so juicy. With everything you learned out there on the battlefield, you now play your trumpet with deeper compassion and a full sense of celebration. Your wings are wide open and you are looking down on the magnificent, majestic, mysterious physical expression of Gaia herself—Planet Earth. She is the one after all that initiated you. She took your wings and lifted them higher. She showed you how to eventually do that for yourself. She looked you straight in the eyes and bowed to you. She bowed down to your feet and you wept in humility and awe. She showed herself to you so that you could see yourself. She comforted you when you needed a rest. She took you for a ride when you needed to play. In her wings, she gave you a Mother, a Best Friend, a Sister, a Soulmate, a Partner in Crime. She told you she is doing this with you no matter what. She showed you loyalty and Truth and honor and reverence. She taught you how to be powerful, how to fly, how to access the keys of life. She played you a song so that you could remember that love is always the key. When you unlocked the door, she closed and locked it behind you so that you could never turn back. She humbled you, terrified you, and shook you by bringing you into the parts of yourself you didn't love yet. By her grace she took everything that never belonged to you in the first place so that with lightness, you'd be ready for the flight ahead.

Can I show you how good it can really be from up here? **Gaia**

Closing: Heart-Centered Enterprise

Dear Entrepreneurs,

I write this to you with the upmost honor for your entities, and for you as the chosen channel.

May you listen to your guidance, even when the rest of the world thinks you're crazy.

May you honor the ever-changing role you'll have while channeling an entity.

May you learn complete Surrender in this process, as it is in Surrender where you *are fully caught*.

May you remember that your life, and your entities, are Sacred.

May you break all the rules, simply because it's way more fun.

May you *just know* that you are so deserving.

May you stay curious and ask a lot of really good questions.

May you be a leader that you are truly proud of by staying in *your alignment*.

May you be open enough to receive the gift of your entity.

May you be still enough to notice the pure magic of the unfolding.

May your relationship to money and funding your vision

be rewarding, renewed where needed, and above all, an example to those around you.

May you be soft enough to receive Mother Earth's support to your nervous system.

May you open your hands, mind and heart to your "spirit-squad" so that you can experience just how supported you truly are.

May your life be badass, fun, creative, and bold.

May you delight in every single moment of the journey.

May you have a bit of urgency in starting, because now is the time.

May you become unattached to the timeline once you begin and may you embody full presence.

May you leave a legacy of love that is here long after you're gone.

May your example BE the invitation.

May you get your medicine to the people.

In delight,

Makenzie

About the Author

Makenzie Marzluff is the Founder of *DELIGHTED BY Desserts* and *KAKAO Ceremonial Drinking Chocolate,* a 501c3 non-profit. Makenzie's dream is to see all businesses operated 100% from the heart. She merges spirituality with grounded leadership and is interested in leaving a legacy of love on this planet for future generations.

Makenzie went from starting her companies on credit cards in 2015 and living in a van, to running a multi-milliondollar business within two years. DELIGHTED BY was coined the fasting growing hummus company in America and has been featured in hundreds of media outlets including *ABC'S Shark Tank, LIVE with Kelly, Cosmopolitan* & *Women's Health.* Makenzie now leads her virtual teams in a completely unconventional way. You can find DELIGHTED BY's high-vibe desserts in thousands of grocery stores across the USA, and KAKAO's products online through on-shore distribution centers in the USA, Canada, Australia/New Zealand, and all of Europe.

Makenzie lives in Maui, HI with her Beloved, Michael, and cat, Mo. To learn more about Makenzie and Michael and their businesses, visit www.makenziemarzluff.com.

Acknowledgements

T hank you to every entrepreneur that has already received my message and reflected back to me how much the world is ready for it. It is because of you that I was able to stay motivated enough to actually finish writing this book.

Thank you to *Changemakers Books,* the entity, for encouraging your Chief Channeler, Tim Ward, to publish my book. Thank you, Tim, for having the charisma and heart to ask your entity its opinion in the first place. Tim, your belief in both Michael and me from the beginning was and is an incredible blessing. Thank you for trusting me despite my stubbornness and for letting me challenge you. It has been such a privilege to work with you, with Changemakers, and with the John Hunt Publishing team in bringing this book to physical life.

To my friend Alexis Sones, thank you for bringing your genius and codes through to create the most energetically potent book cover this planet has ever seen. To my friend and business partner, Aydin Rahmi, thank you for doing the hard work of finding us a publisher (you are magic) and for supporting me in bringing this message to life every step of the way. To Maria Dunlevy, thank you for your significant contribution to the finance chapter. To Caitlin Grace @caitlingracephoto, thank you for the heart and energy you poured into my photography for the book's launch.

To all of our tribe—our friends, family, team members, spirit guides and plant helpers—thank you for celebrating, encouraging and contributing to Michael and me through our entire writing and publication process—there are way too many to name, but you know who you are.

To Sozie, thank you for knowing that I was going to write a book before I even did, for being the most consistent voice in my ear, "write the book," for all the words you said that instilled confidence in me, and so much more.

To my beloved, Michael, thank you for reminding me that this book is worth publishing every time I got discouraged, for challenging me to bring it forward in a timely manner, for keeping me sane and smiley through it all, for reflecting back to me how loved and supported I am, and for purchasing Microsoft Word in 2018 (even though I made fun of you for it at the time) so that you could properly format my horribly messy manuscript as per our publisher's standards. If it wasn't for you, I would have legitimately copied and pasted this entire text into a free blog post on my website and called it a day. I love you so damn much.

To DB, thank you for giving me around 67,000 words of content and the wildest journey of my life to date. The next 200 pages are basically just me gushing on you... you're welcome. There is a chapter missing, though. You know what I'm talking about. I'll take it when you're ready, and yet I'm going to miss you like hell. LY.

CHANGEMAKERS
BOOKS

TRANSFORMATION

Transform your life, transform your world - Changemakers Books publishes for individuals committed to transforming their lives and transforming the world. Our readers seek to become positive, powerful agents of change. Changemakers Books inform, inspire, and provide practical wisdom and skills to empower us to write the next chapter of humanity's future. If you have enjoyed this book, why not tell other readers by posting a review on your preferred book site.

Recent bestsellers from Changemakers Books are:

Integration
The Power of Being Co-Active in Work and Life
Ann Betz, Karen Kimsey-House
Integration examines how we came to be polarized in our dealing with self and other, and what we can do to move from an either/ or state to a more effective and fulfilling way of being.
Paperback: 978-1-78279-865-1 ebook: 978-1-78279-866-8

Bleating Hearts
The Hidden World of Animal Suffering
Mark Hawthorne
An investigation of how animals are exploited for entertainment, apparel, research, military weapons, sport, art, religion, food, and more.
Paperback: 978-1-78099-851-0 ebook: 978-1-78099-850-3

Lead Yourself First!
Indispensable Lessons in Business and in Life
Michelle Ray
Are you ready to become the leader of your own life? Apply simple, powerful strategies to take charge of yourself, your career, your destiny.
Paperback: 978-1-78279-703-6 ebook: 978-1-78279-702-9

Burnout to Brilliance
Strategies for Sustainable Success
Jayne Morris
Routinely running on reserves? This book helps you transform your life from burnout to brilliance with strategies for sustainable success.
Paperback: 978-1-78279-439-4 ebook: 978-1-78279-438-7

Goddess Calling
Inspirational Messages & Meditations of Sacred Feminine
Liberation Thealogy
Rev. Dr. Karen Tate
A book of messages and meditations using Goddess archetypes
and mythologies, aimed at educating and inspiring those with
the desire to incorporate a feminine face of God into their
spirituality.
Paperback: 978-1-78279-442-4 ebook: 978-1-78279-441-7

The Master Communicator's Handbook
Teresa Erickson, Tim Ward
Discover how to have the most communicative impact in this
guide by professional communicators with over 30 years of
experience advising leaders of global organizations.
Paperback: 978-1-78535-153-2 ebook: 978-1-78535-154-9

Meditation in the Wild
Buddhism's Origin in the Heart of Nature
Charles S. Fisher Ph.D.
A history of Raw Nature as the Buddha's first teacher, inspiring
some followers to retreat there in search of truth.
Paperback: 978-1-78099-692-9 ebook: 978-1-78099-691-2

Ripening Time
Inside Stories for Aging with Grace
Sherry Ruth Anderson
Ripening Time gives us an indispensable guidebook for growing
into the deep places of wisdom as we age.
Paperback: 978-1-78099-963-0 ebook: 978-1-78099-962-3

Striking at the Roots
A Practical Guide to Animal Activism
Mark Hawthorne
A manual for successful animal activism from an author with
first-hand experience speaking out on behalf of animals.
Paperback: 978-1-84694-091-0 ebook: 978-1-84694-653-0

Readers of ebooks can buy or view any of these bestsellers by
clicking on the live link in the title. Most titles are published
in paperback and as an ebook. Paperbacks are available in
traditional bookshops. Both print and ebook formats are available
online.

Find more titles and sign up to our readers' newsletter at
http://www.johnhuntpublishing.com/transformation
Follow us on Facebook at
https://www.facebook.com/Changemakersbooks